Securities Regulation

Seventh Edition

2016 Case Supplement

2016 Case Supplement

Securities Regulation

Cases and Materials

Seventh Edition

James D. Cox
Brainerd Currie Professor of Law
Duke University

Robert W. Hillman
Professor of Law and Fair Business Practices Chair
University of California, Davis

Donald C. Langevoort
Thomas Aquinas Reynolds Professor of Law
Georgetown University

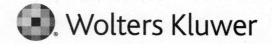

About Wolters Kluwer Legal & Regulatory US

Wolters Kluwer Legal & Regulatory US delivers expert content and solutions in the areas of law, corporate compliance, health compliance, reimbursement, and legal education. Its practical solutions help customers successfully navigate the demands of a changing environment to drive their daily activities, enhance decision quality and inspire confident outcomes.

Serving customers worldwide, its legal and regulatory portfolio includes products under the Aspen Publishers, CCH Incorporated, Kluwer Law International, ftwilliam.com and MediRegs names. They are regarded as exceptional and trusted resources for general legal and practice-specific knowledge, compliance and risk management, dynamic workflow solutions, and expert commentary.

Contents

‖ 6 ‖

Secondary Distributions 85

‖ 8 ‖

Exempt Securities 89

‖ 9 ‖

Liability Under the Securities Act 91

‖10‖

Financial Innovation: Trading Markets, Derivatives, and Securitization 93

‖11‖

Financial Reporting: Mechanisms, Duties and Culture 97

‖12‖

‖13‖

‖14‖

||15||

||16||

||18||

||20||

Table of Cases

||4||

The Public Offering

B. *The Market for Initial Public Offerings*

2. Underpricing of Initial Public Offerings

Page 133.   Add the following at the end of the first paragraph:

Goldman Sachs ultimately paid $7.5 million to settle claims of underpricing the eToy IPO. See http://www.chicagotribune.com/business/sns-rt-us-goldmansachs-etoys

C. *A Panoramic View of the Registration Statement*

Page 136.   At the end of the section, insert the following edited registration statement to illustrate the fruits of the registration process:

S-1 Registration Statement for Weight Watchers International, Inc.

SECURITIES AND EXCHANGE COMMISSION
WASHINGTON, D.C. 20549

FORM S-1

REGISTRATION STATEMENT
UNDER
THE SECURITIES ACT OF 1933

WEIGHT WATCHERS INTERNATIONAL, INC.

VIRGINIA   **7299**   **11-6040273**

175 CROSSWAYS PARK WEST
WOODBURY, NEW YORK 11797-2055
(516) 390-1400

ROBERT HOLLWEG, ESQ.
WEIGHT WATCHERS INTERNATIONAL, INC.
175 CROSSWAYS PARK WEST
WOODBURY, NEW YORK 11797-2055
(516) 390-1400
WITH COPIES TO:

RISE B. NORMAN, ESQ.	KRIS F. HEINZELMAN, ESQ.
SIMPSON THACHER & BARTLETT	CRAVATH, SWAINE & MOORE
425 LEXINGTON AVENUE	825 EIGHTH AVENUE
NEW YORK, NEW YORK 10017	NEW YORK, NEW YORK 10019

3

APPROXIMATE DATE OF COMMENCEMENT OF PROPOSED SALE TO THE PUBLIC: As soon as practicable after this registration statement becomes effective.

If any of the securities being registered on this Form are to be offered on a delayed or continuous basis pursuant to Rule 415 under the Securities Act of 1933, check the following box. ☐

If this Form is filed to register additional securities for an offering pursuant to Rule 462(b) under the Securities Act, please check the following box. ☐

If this Form is a post-effective amendment filed pursuant to Rule 462(c) under the Securities Act, check the following box and list the Securities Act registration statement number of the earlier effective registration statement for the same offering. ☐

_____

If this Form is a post-effective amendment filed pursuant to Rule 462(d) under the Securities Act, check the following box and list the Securities Act registration statement number of the earlier effective registration statement for the same offering. ☐

_____

If delivery of the prospectus is expected to be made pursuant to Rule 434, please check the following box. ☐

_____

CALCULATION OF REGISTRATION FEE

TITLE OF EACH CLASS OF SECURITIES TO BE REGISTERED	AMOUNT TO BE REGISTERED[1]	PROPOSED MAXIMUM OFFERING PRICE PER UNIT	PROPOSED AGGREGATE OFFERING PRICE[2]	AMOUNT OF REGISTRATION FEE[3]
Common stock, no par value	20,010,000 shares	$25.00	$500,250,000	$10,005
Preferred stock purchase rights[4] . . .	—	—	—	—
Total	20,010,000 shares	$25.00	$500,250,000	$10,005

[1] Includes 2,610,000 shares subject to the underwriters' over-allotment option.

[2] Estimated solely for the purpose of calculating the amount of the registration fee pursuant to Rule 457(o).

[3] $25,000 of the total registration fee of $125,063 was paid on September 13, 2001, prior to the initial filing of the registration statement. $90,058 of the total registration fee of $125,063 was paid on October 29, 2001, prior to the filing of Amendment No. 1 to the registration statement. Therefore, the total registration fee payable upon the filing of this Amendment No. 3, calculated in accordance with Rule 457(a), is $10,005.

[4] The preferred stock purchase rights initially will trade together with the common stock. The value attributable to the preferred stock purchase rights, if any, is reflected in the offering price of the common stock.

_____

THE REGISTRANT HEREBY AMENDS THIS REGISTRATION STATEMENT ON SUCH DATE OR DATES AS MAY BE NECESSARY TO DELAY ITS EFFECTIVE DATE UNTIL THE REGISTRANT SHALL FILE A FURTHER AMENDMENT WHICH SPECIFICALLY STATES THAT THIS REGISTRATION STATEMENT SHALL THEREAFTER BECOME EFFECTIVE IN ACCORDANCE WITH SECTION 8(A) OF THE SECURITIES ACT OF 1933 OR UNTIL THE REGISTRATION STATEMENT

SHALL BECOME EFFECTIVE ON SUCH DATE AS THE COMMISSION, ACTING PURSUANT TO SAID SECTION 8(A), MAY DETERMINE.

THE INFORMATION IN THIS PROSPECTUS IS NOT COM-PLETE AND MAY BE CHANGED. WE MAY NOT SELL THESE SECU-RITIES UNTIL THE REGISTRATION STATEMENT FILED WITH THE SECURITIES AND EXCHANGE COMMISSION IS EFFECTIVE. THIS PROSPECTUS IS NOT AN OFFER TO SELL THESE SECU-RITIES AND IT IS NOT SOLICITING AN OFFER TO BUY THESE SECURITIES IN ANY STATE WHERE THE OFFER OR SALE IS NOT PERMITTED.

SUBJECT TO COMPLETION, DATED NOVEMBER 14, 2001

17,400,000 Shares

[LOGO]
Common Stock

The shares of common stock are being sold by the selling share-holders named in this prospectus. We will not receive any of the proceeds from the shares of common stock sold by the selling shareholders.

Prior to this offering, there has been no public market for our common stock. The initial public offering price of the common stock is expected to be between $23.00 and $25.00 per share. Our common stock has been authorized for listing on the New York Stock Exchange under the symbol "WTW."

The underwriters have an option to purchase a maximum of 2,610,000 additional shares from certain of the selling shareholders to cover over-allotments of shares.

Investing in our common stock involves risks. See "Risk Factors" beginning on page 8.

	Price to Public	Underwriting Discounts and Commissions	Proceeds to Selling Shareholders
Per Share	$	$	$
Total	$	$	$

Delivery of the shares of common stock will be made on or about 2001.

Neither the Securities and Exchange Commission nor any state securities commission has approved or disapproved of these securities or determined if this prospectus is truthful or complete. Any representation to the contrary is a criminal offense.

Credit Suisse First Boston   Goldman, Sachs & Co.
Merrill Lynch & Co.
Salomon Smith Barney   UBS Warburg

The date of this prospectus is ⸺⸺⸺.

Picture of Weight Watchers Magazine Cover
Picture of Classroom Meeting
Weight Watchers Logo
Picture of Program Materials
Picture of Program Materials
Picture of Woman Measuring Weight Loss
Picture of Woman Measuring Weight Loss
Picture of Spokeswoman at a Press Conference

―――――――――

TABLE OF CONTENTS

YOU SHOULD RELY ONLY ON THE INFORMATION CON-
TAINED IN THIS DOCUMENT OR TO WHICH WE HAVE REFERRED
YOU. WE HAVE NOT AUTHORIZED ANYONE TO PROVIDE YOU
WITH INFORMATION THAT IS DIFFERENT. THIS DOCUMENT
MAY BE USED ONLY WHERE IT IS LEGAL TO SELL THESE SECU-
RITIES. THE INFORMATION IN THIS DOCUMENT IS ACCURATE
ONLY ON THE DATE OF THIS DOCUMENT.

In this prospectus, "Weight Watchers," "we," "us" and "our" refer to
Weight Watchers International, Inc. and its subsidiaries, unless the context otherwise requires. We refer to our classroom operations that are run
directly by us as company-owned and those run by our franchisees as
franchised. Unless otherwise indicated, the information in this prospectus
assumes the completion of the 4.70536-for-one split of our common stock
that will occur prior to the completion of this offering.

In January 2001, we acquired the business of one of our two largest
franchisees, Weighco Enterprises, Inc. and its subsidiaries, which we
collectively refer to as Weighco. When we state that information is presented on a pro forma basis, we have taken into account the Weighco
acquisition on the pro forma basis described under "Pro Forma Combined Financial Information."

UNTIL _____, 2001 (25 DAYS AFTER THE COMMENCE-
MENT OF THE OFFERING), ALL DEALERS THAT EFFECT
TRANSACTIONS IN THESE SECURITIES, WHETHER OR NOT
PARTICIPATING IN THIS OFFERING, MAY BE REQUIRED TO
DELIVER A PROSPECTUS. THIS IS IN ADDITION TO THE
DEALER'S OBLIGATION TO DELIVER A PROSPECTUS WHEN
ACTING AS AN UNDERWRITER AND WITH RESPECT TO UNSOLD
ALLOTMENTS OR SUBSCRIPTIONS.

PROSPECTUS SUMMARY

THIS SUMMARY HIGHLIGHTS INFORMATION CONTAINED
ELSEWHERE IN THIS PROSPECTUS IS NOT COMPLETE AND MAY
NOT CONTAIN ALL THE INFORMATION THAT MAY BE IMPOR-
TANT TO YOU. YOU SHOULD READ THE ENTIRE PROSPEC-
TUS BEFORE MAKING AN INVESTMENT DECISION, ESPECIALLY
THE INFORMATION PRESENTED UNDER THE HEADING "RISK
FACTORS."

WEIGHT WATCHERS

We are a leading global branded consumer company and the leading provider of weight-loss services in 27 countries around the world. Our programs help people lose weight and maintain their weight loss and, as a result, improve their health, enhance their lifestyles and build self-confidence. At the core of our business are weekly meetings, which promote weight loss through education and group support in conjunction with a flexible, healthy diet. Each week more than one million members attend approximately 37,000 Weight Watchers meetings, which are run by over 13,000 classroom leaders. Our classroom leaders teach, inspire, motivate and act as role models for our members. Our members typically enroll to attend consecutive weekly meetings and have historically demonstrated a consistent re-enrollment pattern across many years.

We have experienced strong growth in sales and profits over the last five years since we made the strategic decision to re-focus our meetings exclusively on our group education approach. We discontinued the in-meeting sale of pre-packaged meals added in 1990 in our North America company-owned operations by our previous owner, Heinz. We also modernized our diet to adapt it to contemporary lifestyles. Through these initiatives, combined with our strengthened management and strategic focus since our acquisition by Artal Luxembourg, we have grown our attendance at a compound annual rate of approximately 13% from fiscal 1997 through 2000 and our operating profit margin improved from 6.7% (before a restructuring charge) to 25.9% over the same period. . . .

The number of overweight and obese people worldwide has been increasing due to improving living standards and changing eating patterns, as well as increasingly sedentary lifestyles. The proportion of U.S. adults who are overweight has grown from 47% to 61% over the last 20 years, and the number of overweight people worldwide now exceeds one billion. A growing number of overweight people are dieting not only because of a desire to improve their appearance but also due to a greater awareness of the health risks associated with being overweight.

Throughout our 40-year history, we have maintained that long-term behavior modification is the only effective way to achieve sustainable weight loss. Although approximately 70% of U.S. dieters try to lose weight by themselves, clinical studies have shown that people who attend Weight Watchers meetings are much more likely to lose weight than people who diet on their own. In contrast to our group education approach to long-term behavior modification, most weight-loss companies have focused on quick-fix methods, such as fad diets, meal replacements and diet drugs, and have typically experienced limited or short-lived success. We believe that our approach will continue to achieve success and that we will capture an increasing share of the growing worldwide market for weight-loss services.

OUR STRENGTHS

— BILLION DOLLAR GLOBAL BRAND. Our proven 40-year track record of safe and sensible weight loss has established WEIGHT WATCHERS as the leading global weight-loss brand. We believe that our brand conveys an image of effective, healthy and flexible weight loss in a supportive environment. Our brand is widely recognized throughout the world with retail sales of over $1.5 billion in 2000, including sales by licensees and franchisees. Currently, over 97% of U.S. women recognize the WEIGHT WATCHERS brand. . . .

— LEADING MARKET POSITION. We are the market leader in weight-loss services in every country in which we operate, other than Denmark, Poland and South Africa. . . .

— LOYAL MEMBER BASE. For many of our members, our classroom program is an inspirational experience that helps them address their life-long challenge of weight control. Our members have historically demonstrated a consistent pattern of repeat enrollment over a number of years. On average, in our North America company-owned, or NACO, operations, our members have enrolled in four separate program cycles.

— ATTRACTIVE VALUE TO MEMBERS. Our low meeting fees ($10 in our NACO operations) offer members an attractive value as compared to other alternatives. For their fee, our members gain access to our scientifically developed diet, detailed program materials and class instruction by one of our trained leaders, as well as group support where members contribute to each other's weight-loss success.

— UNIQUE BUSINESS MODEL. Our business model features high margins, a variable cost structure and low capital requirements.

— HIGH CONTRIBUTION MARGINS. During 2000, our meetings generated a contribution margin of approximately 50%. In that period, for example, our NACO meetings averaged attendance of 34 members and generated average revenues of over $440 per class, including product sales, while our cost of sales is primarily the compensation of two or three part-time employees, the hourly rental of the meeting location and the cost of products sold.

— VARIABLE COST STRUCTURE. Our staff is usually paid on a commission basis and space is typically rented as needed. Moreover, we adjust the number of meetings according to demand, including seasonal fluctuations. This variable cost structure enables us to maintain high margins across varying levels of demand.

9

— LOW MARKETING COSTS. Our marketing expenditures were less than 15% of our revenues in 2000. Our strong brand, together with the effectiveness of our program and our loyal member base, enable us to attract new and returning members efficiently through both word-of-mouth referrals and mass marketing programs.

— STRONG FREE CASH FLOW. In 2000, our operating income margin was over 25%, while our capital expenditures were less than 1% of revenues. Because we can add additional meetings with little or no capital expenditures and our members typically pay cash at each meeting or prepay for a series of meetings, we require little new capital to grow.

OUR GROWTH STRATEGY

The large and growing global weight-loss market provides us with significant growth potential. In addition, we believe we can increase our share of this market by:

— INCREASING PENETRATION IN EXISTING MAJOR MARKETS. In the United Kingdom, the penetration rate of our target demographic group, overweight women ages 25 to 64, by all group education-based commercial weight-loss programs now exceeds 20%. We believe that this demonstrates the potential for significant increases in penetration in our other major markets. Because we do not face significant group education-based competition outside the United Kingdom, we believe that we are best positioned to capture this growth. . . .

— DEVELOPING LESS PENETRATED MARKETS AND ENTERING NEW MARKETS. We believe that we have significant long-term growth opportunities in countries where we have established a meeting infrastructure but where our penetration rates are relatively low. For example, in Germany, we have grown attendance by over 65% in the twelve months ended September 29, 2001, while still penetrating less than 2% of our target market. . . .

— GROWING PRODUCT SALES. In 2000, sales of our proprietary products represented 26% of our revenues, up from 11% in fiscal 1997. We have grown our product sales per attendance by focusing on a core group of products that complement our program. We currently sell snack bars, books, CD-ROMs, POINTS calculators and other items primarily through classroom operations. We will continue to optimize our classroom product offerings by updating existing products and selectively introducing new products.

— GROWING LICENSING ROYALTIES. We currently license the WEIGHT WATCHERS brand in certain categories of food, apparel, books and other products. We derived less than 2% of our 2000 revenues from licensing and royalties but believe there are opportunities

to take fuller advantage of the strength of our brand through additional licensing agreements. . . .
— ADDRESSING NEW CUSTOMER SEGMENTS. We believe there are significant opportunities to expand our customer base by developing products and services designed to meet the needs of a broader audience. . . .

RECENT DEVELOPMENTS

On October 29, 2001, we reported net revenues for the three months and nine months ended September 29, 2001 of $144.0 million and $478.3 million, respectively. Our net revenues for the three months and nine months ended September 29, 2001 increased 19.4% and 25.2% compared with pro forma net revenues for the comparable prior year periods. Our operating income for the three months and nine months ended September 29, 2001 was $50.9 million and $160.0 million, respectively. Our operating income for the three months and nine months ended September 29, 2001 increased 63.5% and 46.5% compared with pro forma operating income for the comparable prior year periods.

The increases in our revenues and profitability reflect the continuing strong growth in attendance and product sales across our major markets. Attendance was 10.8 million for the quarter ended September 29, 2001, an increase from pro forma attendance of 9.1 million for the three months ended September 30, 2000. . . .

We are a Virginia corporation incorporated in 1974. Our principal executive offices are located at 175 Crossways Park West, Woodbury, New York 11797-2055. Our telephone number at that address is (516) 390-1400.

THE OFFERING

Common stock offered by the selling shareholders	17,400,000 shares (or 20,010,000 shares if the underwriters exercise the over-allotment option in full)
Total common stock outstanding after this offering	105,407,142 shares
Use of proceeds	We will not receive any of the proceeds from the sale of shares by the selling shareholders. The selling shareholders will receive all net proceeds from the sale of shares of our common stock offered in this prospectus.
Dividend policy	We do not expect to pay any dividends on our common stock for the foreseeable future.
New York Stock Exchange symbol.	WTW

11

The number of shares of common stock shown to be outstanding after this offering is based on the number of shares outstanding as of September 29, 2001. This number excludes:

— 5,763,692 shares of our common stock issuable upon exercise of outstanding stock options and

— 1,294,348 shares of our common stock reserved for future issuance under our existing stock option plan.

SUMMARY PRO FORMA COMBINED FINANCIAL INFORMATION

The summary pro forma combined financial information has been derived from the unaudited pro forma combined statements of operations and the related note included elsewhere in this prospectus, which give effect to our acquisition on January 16, 2001 of the franchised territories and certain business assets of Weighco for $83.8 million and the related financing of the acquisition. We financed the acquisition with available cash of $23.8 million and additional borrowings of $60.0 million under our senior credit facilities. . . .

Effective April 30, 2000, we changed our fiscal year end from the last Saturday in April to the Saturday closest to December 31. As a result of this change in our reporting period, the significant growth in our business since the fiscal year ended April 29, 2000 and the Weighco acquisition, we have included unaudited pro forma combined results of operations for the twelve months ended December 30, 2000. Given these events, we believe the pro forma results of operations for the twelve months ended December 30, 2000 are more indicative of our current operations. Our results of operations for the twelve months ended December 30, 2000 have been derived from our historical results for the eight months ended December 30, 2000, plus our results for the four months ended April 29, 2000, which are derived from our results for the historical fiscal year ended April 29, 2000. We have included a comparison of the nine months ended September 29, 2001 to the nine months ended October 28, 2000, which, in the opinion of our management, is the available period most comparable to the nine months ended September 29, 2001.

SUMMARY PRO FORMA COMBINED FINANCIAL INFORMATION

	FISCAL YEAR ENDED APRIL 29, 2000	TWELVE MONTHS ENDED DECEMBER 30, 2000	NINE MONTHS ENDED OCTOBER 28, 2000	NINE MONTHS ENDED SEPTEMBER 29, 2001
	(53 weeks)	(54 weeks)	(40 weeks)	(39 weeks)
		(in millions, except per share amounts)		
STATEMENT OF OPERATIONS INFORMATION:				
Revenues, net	$436.4	$488.2	$382.1	$480.1
Cost of revenues	216.8	237.5	183.3	215.6
Gross profit	219.6	250.7	198.8	264.5
Marketing expenses	55.0	58.9	40.3	51.8
Selling, general and administrative expenses.......	60.3	62.7	49.3	51.9
Transaction costs................	8.3	—	—	—
Operating income...............	96.0	129.1	109.2	160.8
Interest expense, net...........	40.1	66.8	49.9	42.3
Other (income) expense, net	(10.5)	7.6	(6.7)	13.9
Income before income taxes and minority interest	66.4	54.7	66.0	104.6
Provision for income taxes	28.1	20.1	21.3	38.8
Income before minority interest	38.3	34.6	44.7	65.8
Minority interest	0.8	0.3	0.2	0.1
Net income	$ 37.5	$ 34.3	$ 44.5	$ 65.7
Preferred stock dividends	$ 0.9	$ 1.5	$ 1.1	$ 1.1
Net income available to common shareholders	$ 36.6	$ 32.8	$ 43.4	$ 64.6
PER SHARE INFORMATION:				
Basic earnings per share	0.20	0.29	0.39	0.59
Diluted earnings per share	0.20	0.29	0.39	0.58
Basic weighted average number of shares*	182.1	112.0	112.0	109.8
Diluted weighted average number of shares*	182.1	112.0	112.0	111.4
OTHER FINANCIAL INFORMATION:				
Depreciation and amortization ..	18.1	14.0	11.5	10.0
Capital expenditures	2.7	4.3	2.7	1.9

* Prior to our acquisition by Artal Luxembourg on September 29, 1999, there were 4,705 shares of our common stock outstanding. In connection with the transactions related to our acquisition, we declared a stock split that resulted in 276,428,607 outstanding shares of our common stock. We have adjusted our historical statements to reflect the stock split. We then repurchased 164,441,039 shares in connection with the transactions so that upon completion of our acquisition, there were 111,987,568 shares of our common stock outstanding.

EIGHT

SUMMARY HISTORICAL
CONSOLIDATED FINANCIAL INFORMATION

The following table sets forth certain of our historical financial information. The summary historical consolidated financial information as of and for the fiscal years ended April 25, 1998, April 24, 1999 and April 29, 2000 and the eight months ended December 30, 2000 have been derived from, and should be read in conjunction with, our audited consolidated financial statements and the related notes included elsewhere in this prospectus. The summary historical consolidated financial information as of and for the nine months ended October 28, 2000 and September 29, 2001 have been derived from, and should be read in conjunction with, our unaudited consolidated financial statements and the related notes included elsewhere in this prospectus. Interim results for the nine months ended September 29, 2001 are not necessarily indicative of, and are not projections for, the results to be expected for the full fiscal year.

	FISCAL YEAR ENDED			EIGHT MONTHS ENDED	NINE MONTHS ENDED	
	APRIL 25, 1998	APRIL 24, 1999	APRIL 29, 2000	DEC. 30, 2000	OCT. 28, 2000	SEPT. 29, 2001
	(52 weeks)	(52 weeks)	(53 weeks)	(35 weeks)	(40 weeks)	(39 weeks)
			(in millions, except per share amounts)			
STATEMENT OF OPERATIONS INFORMATION:						
Revenues, net	$297.2	$364.6	$399.5	$273.2	$343.5	$478.3
Cost of revenues	160.0	178.9	201.4	139.3	167.2	215.1
Gross profit	137.2	185.7	198.1	133.9	176.3	263.2
Marketing expenses	49.2	52.9	51.5	27.0	37.1	51.5
Selling, general and administrative expenses	44.1	48.9	50.7	32.2	40.8	51.7
Transaction costs	—	—	8.3	—	—	—
Operating income	43.9	83.9	87.6	74.7	98.4	160.0
Interest (income) expense, net	(4.9)	(7.1)	31.1	37.1	42.9	42.0
Other expense (income), net	4.3	5.2	(10.4)	16.5	(6.7)	13.9
Income before income taxes and minority interest	44.5	85.8	66.9	21.1	62.2	104.1
Provision for income taxes	19.9	36.4	28.3	5.9	19.9	38.6
Income before minority interest	24.6	49.4	38.6	15.2	42.3	65.5
Minority interest	0.8	1.5	0.8	0.2	0.2	0.1
Net income	$ 23.8	$ 47.9	$ 37.8	$ 15.0	$ 42.1	$ 65.4
Preferred stock dividends	—	—	$ 0.9	$ 1.0	$ 1.1	$ 1.1
Net income available to common shareholders	$ 23.8	$ 47.9	$ 36.9	$ 14.0	$ 41.0	$ 64.3

PER SHARE INFORMATION:

Basic earnings per share	$ 0.09	$ 0.17	$ 0.20	$ 0.13	$ 0.37	$ 0.59
Diluted earnings per share	$ 0.09	$ 0.17	$ 0.20	$ 0.13	$ 0.37	$ 0.58
Basic weighted average number of shares*	276.2	276.2	182.1	112.0	112.0	109.8
Diluted weighted average number of shares*	276.2	276.2	182.1	112.0	112.0	111.4

OTHER FINANCIAL INFORMATION:
Net cash provided by (used in):

Operating activities	$ 36.4	$ 57.9	$ 49.9	$ 28.9	$ 50.1	$ 120.2
Investing activities	(4.9)	(3.0)	(19.6)	(21.6)	(15.7)	(110.7)
Financing activities	(30.6)	(47.7)	8.1	(8.0)	(4.7)	(15.5)
Depreciation and amortization ...	8.8	9.6	10.4	7.9	8.5	9.8
Capital expenditures	3.4	2.5	1.9	3.6	2.2	1.9

BALANCE SHEET INFORMATION
(AT END OF PERIOD):

Working capital (deficit)	$ 65.8	$ 91.2	$ (0.9)	$ 10.2	$ 3.3	$ (35.2)
Total assets	370.8	371.4	334.2	346.2	346.9	423.4
Total debt	41.1	39.6	474.6	470.7	460.5	480.8
Redeemable securities:						
Preferred stock	—	—	25.9	26.0	25.7	25.6

*Prior to our acquisition by Artal Luxembourg on September 29,1999, there were 4,705 shares of our common stock outstanding. In connection with the transactions related to our acquisition, we declared a stock split that resulted in 276,428,607 outstanding shares of our common stock. We have adjusted our historical statements to reflect the stock split. We then repurchased 164,441,039 shares in connection with the transactions so that upon completion of our acquisition, there were 111,987,568 shares of our common stock outstanding.

RISK FACTORS

AN INVESTMENT IN OUR COMMON STOCK INVOLVES RISKS. YOU SHOULD CONSIDER CAREFULLY, IN ADDITION TO THE OTHER INFORMATION CONTAINED IN THIS PROSPECTUS, THE FOLLOWING RISK FACTORS BEFORE DECIDING TO PURCHASE ANY SHARES OF OUR COMMON STOCK.

RISKS RELATING TO OUR COMPANY

COMPETITION FROM A VARIETY OF OTHER WEIGHT-LOSS METHODS COULD RESULT IN DECREASED DEMAND FOR OUR SERVICES.

The weight-loss business is highly competitive and we compete against a large number of alternative providers of various sizes, some of which may have greater financial resources than we. We compete against self-administered weight-loss regimens, other commercial weight-loss programs, Internet-based weight-loss programs, nutritionists, dietitians, the pharmaceutical industry, dietary supplements and certain government agencies and non-profit groups that offer weight control help by means of diets, exercise and weight-loss drugs. We also compete against food manufacturers and distributors that are developing and marketing meal replacement and diet products to weight-conscious consumers. In addition, new or different products or methods of weight control are continually being introduced. This competition and any increase in competition, including new pharmaceuticals and other technological and scientific developments in weight control, may result in decreased demand for our services.

OUR OPERATING RESULTS DEPEND ON THE EFFECTIVENESS OF OUR MARKETING AND ADVERTISING PROGRAMS.

Our business success depends on our ability to attract new members to our classes and retain existing members. The effectiveness of our marketing practices, in particular our advertising campaigns, is important to our financial performance. . . .

IF WE DO NOT CONTINUE TO DEVELOP NEW PRODUCTS AND SERVICES AND ENHANCE OUR EXISTING PRODUCTS AND SER-VICES, OUR BUSINESS MAY SUFFER.

Our future success depends on our ability to continue to develop and market new products and services and to enhance our existing products and services on a timely basis to respond to new and evolving customer demands, achieve market acceptance and keep pace with new nutritional and weight-loss developments. We may not be successful in developing, introducing on a timely basis or marketing any new or enhanced products and services, and we cannot assure you that any new or enhanced products or services will be accepted by the market. . . .

OUR DEBT SERVICE OBLIGATIONS COULD IMPEDE OUR OPERA-TIONS AND FLEXIBILITY.

Our financial performance could be affected by our level of debt. As of September 29, 2001, we had total debt and redeemable preferred stock of $506.4 million. . . . Our net interest expense for the eight months ended December 30, 2000 and for the nine months ended September 29, 2001 was $37.1 million and $42.0 million, respectively.

Our level of debt could have important consequences for you, in-cluding the following:

— we will need to use a large portion of the money we earn to pay principal and interest on outstanding amounts due . . . which will reduce the amount of money available to us for financing our operations and other business activities,

— we may have a much higher level of debt than certain of our competitors, which may put us at a competitive disadvantage,

— we may have difficulty borrowing money in the future and

— our debt level makes us more vulnerable to economic downturns and adverse developments in our business. . . .

WE ARE SUBJECT TO RESTRICTIVE DEBT COVENANTS, WHICH MAY RESTRICT OUR OPERATIONAL FLEXIBILITY.

Our senior credit facilities contain covenants that restrict our ability to incur additional indebtedness, pay dividends on and redeem capital stock, make other restricted payments, including investments, sell our assets and enter into consolidations, mergers and transfers of all or substantially all of our assets. Our senior credit facilities also require us to maintain specified financial ratios and satisfy financial condition tests. These tests and financial ratios become more restrictive over the life of the credit facilities. Our ability to meet those financial ratios and tests can be affected by events beyond our control and we cannot assure you that we will meet those ratios and tests. A breach of any of these covenants, ratios, tests or restrictions could result in an event of default under the credit facilities. In an event of default under the credit facilities, the lenders could elect to declare all amounts outstanding thereunder to be immediately due and payable. If the lenders under the credit facilities accelerate the payment of the indebtedness, we cannot assure you that our assets would be sufficient to repay in full that indebtedness and our other indebtedness that would become due as a result of any acceleration. . . .

ACTIONS TAKEN BY OUR FRANCHISEES AND LICENSEES MAY HARM OUR BRAND OR REPUTATION.

We believe that the WEIGHT WATCHERS brand is one of our most valuable assets and that our reputation provides us with a competitive advantage. . . . Because our franchisees and licensees are independent third parties with their own financial objectives, actions taken by them, including breaches of their contractual obligations, such as not following our diets or not maintaining our quality standards, could harm our brand or reputation. Also, the products we license to third parties may be subject to product recalls or other deficiencies. Any negative publicity associated with these actions or recalls may adversely affect our reputation and thereby result in decreased classroom attendance and lower revenues.

DISPUTES WITH OUR FRANCHISE OPERATORS COULD DIVERT OUR MANAGEMENT'S ATTENTION.

In the past, we have had disputes with our franchisees regarding operations and revenue sharing. We continue to have disputes with a few of our franchisees. . . . These disputes and any future disputes could divert the attention of our management from their ordinary responsibilities.

17

OUR INTERNATIONAL OPERATIONS EXPOSE US TO ECONOMIC, POLITICAL AND SOCIAL RISKS IN THE COUNTRIES IN WHICH WE OPERATE.

The international nature of our existing and planned operations involves a number of risks, including changes in U.S. and foreign government regulations, tariffs, taxes and exchange controls, economic downturns, inflation and political and social instability in the countries in which we operate and our dependence on foreign personnel. . . .

WE ARE EXPOSED TO FOREIGN CURRENCY RISKS FROM OUR INTERNATIONAL OPERATIONS THAT COULD ADVERSELY AFFECT OUR FINANCIAL RESULTS.

A significant portion of our revenues and operating costs are, and a portion of our indebtedness is, denominated in foreign currencies. We are therefore exposed to fluctuations in the exchange rates between the U.S. dollar and the currencies in which our foreign operations receive revenues and pay expenses, including debt service. . . .

OUR RESULTS OF OPERATIONS MAY DECLINE AS A RESULT OF A DOWNTURN IN GENERAL ECONOMIC CONDITIONS.

. . . A downturn in general economic conditions or consumer confidence and spending in any of our major markets caused by the recent terrorist attacks or other events outside of our control could result in people curtailing their discretionary spending, which, in turn, could reduce attendance at our meetings. . . .

THE SEASONAL NATURE OF OUR BUSINESS COULD CAUSE OUR OPERATING RESULTS TO FLUCTUATE.

We have experienced and expect to continue to experience fluctuations in our quarterly results of operations. . . . This seasonality could cause our share price to fluctuate as the results of an interim financial period may not be indicative of our full year results. In addition, our classroom operations are subject to local conditions beyond our control, including the weather, natural disasters and other extraordinary events, that may prevent current or prospective members from attending or joining classes. . . .

OUR ADVERTISING AND FRANCHISE OPERATIONS ARE SUBJECT TO LEGISLATIVE AND REGULATORY RESTRICTIONS.

A number of laws and regulations govern our advertising, franchise operations and relations with consumers. The Federal Trade Commission, or FTC, and certain states regulate advertising, disclosures to consumers and franchisees and other consumer matters. Our customers may

18

file actions on their own behalf, as a class or otherwise, and may file complaints with the FTC or state or local consumer affairs offices and these agencies may take action on their own initiative or on a referral from consumers or others.

During the mid-1990s, the FTC filed complaints against a number of commercial weight-loss providers alleging violations of the Federal Trade Commission Act by the use and content of advertisements for weight-loss programs that featured testimonials, claims for program success and safety and statements as to program costs to participants. In 1997, we entered into a consent order with the FTC settling all contested issues raised in the complaint filed against us. The consent order requires us to comply with certain procedures and disclosures in connection with our advertisements of products and services. . . .

RISKS RELATED TO THIS OFFERING

THERE IS NO EXISTING MARKET FOR OUR COMMON STOCK, AND WE DO NOT KNOW IF ONE WILL DEVELOP TO PROVIDE YOU WITH ADEQUATE LIQUIDITY.

There has not been a public market for our common stock. We cannot predict the extent to which investor interest in our company will lead to the development of a trading market on the New York Stock Exchange or otherwise or how liquid that market might become. The initial public offering price for the shares will be determined by negotiations between the selling shareholders and the representatives of the underwriters and may not be indicative of prices that will prevail in the open market following this offering.

ARTAL LUXEMBOURG CONTROLS US AND MAY HAVE CON-FLICTS OF INTEREST WITH OTHER SHAREHOLDERS IN THE FUTURE.

Artal Luxembourg S.A. controls us. After this offering, Artal Luxembourg will beneficially own 78.8% of our common stock or 76.4% if the underwriters exercise their over-allotment option in full. As a result, Artal Luxembourg will continue to be able to control the election and removal of our directors and determine our corporate and management policies, including potential mergers or acquisitions, payment of dividends, asset sales and other significant corporate transactions. We cannot assure you that the interests of Artal Luxembourg will coincide with the interests of other holders of our common stock. In addition, Artal Luxembourg also owns 72.3% of the common stock, or 48.1% on a fully diluted basis, of our licensee, WeightWatchers.com. Artal Luxembourg's interests with respect to WeightWatchers.com may differ from the interests of our other shareholders.

19

FUTURE SALES OF OUR SHARES COULD DEPRESS THE MARKET PRICE OF OUR COMMON STOCK.

The market price of our common stock could decline as a result of sales of a large number of shares of our common stock in the market after this offering or the perception that these sales could occur. . . .

Following this offering, Artal Luxembourg will own 83,062,423 shares of our common stock or 80,517,663 shares if the underwriters exercise their over-allotment option in full. Artal Luxembourg will be able to sell its shares in the public market from time to time, subject to certain limitations on the timing, amount and method of those sales imposed by SEC regulations. Artal Luxembourg and the underwriters have agreed to a "lock-up" period, meaning that Artal Luxembourg may not sell any of its shares without the prior consent of Credit Suisse First Boston Corporation for 180 days after the date of this prospectus. Artal Luxembourg has the right to cause us to register the sale of shares of common stock owned by it and to include its shares in future registration statements relating to our securities. If Artal Luxembourg were to sell a large number of its shares, the market price of our stock could decline significantly. In addition, the perception in the public markets that sales by Artal Luxembourg might occur could also adversely affect the market price of our common stock.

In addition to Artal Luxembourg's lock-up period, sales of our common stock are also restricted by lock-up agreements that our directors and executive officers and the selling shareholders have entered into with the underwriters. . . .

OUR ARTICLES OF INCORPORATION AND BYLAWS AND VIRGINIA CORPORATE LAW CONTAIN PROVISIONS THAT MAY DISCOURAGE A TAKEOVER ATTEMPT.

Provisions contained in our articles of incorporation and bylaws and the laws of Virginia, the state in which we are organized, could make it more difficult for a third party to acquire us, even if doing so might be beneficial to our shareholders. . . . For example, our articles of incorporation authorize our board of directors to determine the rights, preferences, privileges and restrictions of unissued series of preferred stock, without any vote or action by our shareholders. Thus, our board of directors can authorize and issue shares of preferred stock with voting or conversion rights that could adversely affect the voting or other rights of holders of our common stock. . . .

THE MARKET PRICE OF OUR COMMON STOCK MAY BE VOLATILE, WHICH COULD CAUSE THE VALUE OF YOUR INVESTMENT TO DECLINE.

Securities markets worldwide experience significant price and volume fluctuations. . . . In addition, our operating results could be below the expectations of public market analysts and investors, and in response, the market price of our common stock could decrease significantly. You may be unable to resell your shares of our common stock at or above the initial public offering price.

CAUTIONARY NOTICE
REGARDING FORWARD-LOOKING STATEMENTS

This prospectus includes forward-looking statements including, in particular, the statements about our plans, strategies and prospects under the headings "Prospectus Summary," "Management's Discussion and Analysis of Financial Condition and Results of Operations," "Industry" and "Business." We have used the words "may," "will," "expect," "anticipate," "believe," "estimate," "plan," "intend" and similar expressions in this prospectus to identify forward-looking statements. . . . Actual results could differ materially from those projected in the forward-looking statements. These forward-looking statements are subject to risks, uncertainties and assumptions, including, among other things:

— competition, including price competition and competition with self-help, medical and other weight-loss programs and products;
— risks associated with the relative success of our marketing and advertising;
— risks associated with the continued attractiveness of our programs;
— risks associated with our ability to meet our obligations related to our outstanding indebtedness;
— risks associated with general economic conditions;
— adverse results in litigation and regulatory matters, the adoption of adverse legislation or regulations, more aggressive enforcement of existing legislation or regulations or a change in the interpretation of existing legislation or regulations; and
— the other factors referenced under the heading "Risk Factors."

You should not put undue reliance on any forward-looking statements. You should understand that many important factors, including those discussed under the headings "Risk Factors" and "Management's Discussion and Analysis of Financial Conditions and Results of Operations," could cause our results to differ materially from those expressed or suggested in any forward-looking statements.

USE OF PROCEEDS

We will not receive any of the proceeds from the sale of shares by the selling shareholders. The selling shareholders will receive all net proceeds from the sale of the shares of our common stock in this offering.

DIVIDEND POLICY

We do not intend to pay any dividends on our common stock in the foreseeable future. . . .

CAPITALIZATION

The following table sets forth our cash and our capitalization as of September 29, 2001. You should read this table in conjunction with our consolidated financial statements and the related notes included elsewhere in this prospectus. . . .

SEPTEMBER 29, 2001

	(in millions)
Cash	$ 37.9
Long-term debt (including current maturities):	
Senior credit facilities	$ 239.6
Senior subordinated notes due 2009	241.2
Total long-term debt	480.8
Redeemable preferred stock	25.6
Shareholders' deficit:	
Common stock, no par value (1,000,000,000 authorized, 111,987,568 issued and 105,407,142 outstanding)...................	—
Treasury stock, at cost, 6,580,426 shares	(26.6)
Accumulated (deficit)	(152.2)
Accumulated other comprehensive (loss)	(15.3)
Total shareholders' (deficit)	(194.1)
Total capitalization	$ 312.3

PRO FORMA COMBINED FINANCIAL INFORMATION

On January 16, 2001, we acquired the franchised territories and certain business assets, including inventory, property and equipment, of Weighco for $83.8 million. . . . The acquisition has been accounted for under the purchase method of accounting and, accordingly, the results of operations of Weighco are included from the date of acquisition. . . .

The unaudited pro forma combined statements of operations give effect to the Weighco acquisition and the related financing as if each had occurred on April 25, 1999. . . .

Effective April 30, 2000, we changed our fiscal year end from the last Saturday in April to the Saturday closest to December 31. As a result of this change in our reporting period, the significant growth in our business since the fiscal year ended April 29, 2000 and the Weighco acquisition, we have included unaudited pro forma combined results of operations for the twelve months ended December 30, 2000. Given these events, we believe the pro forma results of operations for the twelve months ended December 30, 2000 are more indicative of our current operations. We have included a comparison of the nine months ended September 29, 2001 to the nine months ended October 28, 2000, which, in the opinion of our management, is the available period most comparable to the nine months ended September 29, 2001. . . .

PRO FORMA COMBINED STATEMENT OF OPERATIONS FOR THE TWELVE MONTHS ENDED DECEMBER 30, 2000 (UNAUDITED)

[Pro Forma Statements Omitted: Eds.]

SELECTED HISTORICAL FINANCIAL AND OTHER INFORMATION

The following table sets forth our selected historical financial and other information and the related notes. . . .

	FISCAL YEAR ENDED				
	APRIL 27, 1996 (52 weeks)	APRIL 26, 1997 (52 weeks)	APRIL 25, 1998 (52 weeks)	APRIL 24, 1999 (52 weeks)	APRIL 29, 2000 (53 weeks)
		(in millions, except per share amounts)			
STATEMENT OF OPERATIONS INFORMATION:					
Revenues, net	$ 323.3	$ 292.8	$ 297.2	$ 364.6	$ 399.5
Cost of revenues...........................	190.9	230.4(1)	160.0	178.9	201.4
Gross profit	132.4	62.4	137.2	185.7	198.1
Marketing expenses	53.9	48.9	49.2	52.9	51.5
Selling, general and administrative expenses	51.9	45.5(1)	44.1	48.9	50.7
Transaction costs	—	—	—	—	8.3
Operating income (loss)	26.6	(32.0)	43.9	83.9	87.6
Interest expense (income), net	3.3	1.0	(4.9)	(7.1)	31.1
Other expense (income), net	4.8	3.3	4.3	5.2	(10.4)
Income (loss) before income taxes and minority interests	18.5	(36.3)	44.5	85.8	66.9
(Benefit from) provision for income taxes...	(3.6)	(12.9)	19.9	36.4	28.3
Income (loss) before minority interests ...	22.1	(23.4)	24.6	49.4	38.6
Minority interest	0.6	0.6	0.8	1.5	0.8
Net income (loss)	$ 21.5	$ (24.0)	$ 23.8	$ 47.9	$ 37.8
Preferred stock dividends	—	—	—	—	$ 0.9
Net income (loss) available to common shareholders	$ 21.5	$ (24.0)	$ 23.8	147.9	$ 36.9

[Schedule of 8 Month and 9 Month Financial Performance Omitted: eds.]

MANAGEMENT'S DISCUSSION AND ANALYSIS OF
FINANCIAL CONDITION AND RESULTS OF OPERATIONS

YOU SHOULD READ THE FOLLOWING DISCUSSION IN CONJUNCTION WITH "SELECTED HISTORICAL FINANCIAL AND OTHER INFORMATION" AND OUR CONSOLIDATED FINANCIAL STATEMENTS AND RELATED NOTES INCLUDED ELSEWHERE IN THIS PROSPECTUS. UNLESS OTHERWISE NOTED, REFERENCES TO THE 1997, 1998, 1999 AND 2000 FISCAL YEARS ARE TO OUR FISCAL YEARS ENDED APRIL 26, 1997, APRIL 25, 1998, APRIL 24, 1999 AND APRIL 29, 2000, RESPECTIVELY. AFTER THE FISCAL YEAR ENDED APRIL 29, 2000, WE CHANGED OUR FISCAL YEAR END TO THE SATURDAY CLOSEST TO DECEMBER 31. ACCORDINGLY, THE FISCAL YEAR ENDED DECEMBER 30, 2000 IS AN EIGHT-MONTH PERIOD.

OVERVIEW

We are the leading provider of weight-loss services in 27 countries around the world. We conduct our business through a combination of company-owned and franchise operations, with company-owned operations accounting for 65% of total worldwide attendance in the first nine months of 2001. For the first nine months of 2001, 63% of our revenues were derived from our U.S. operations, and the remaining 37% of our revenues were derived from our international operations. We derive our revenues principally from:

— MEETING FEES. . . .
— PRODUCT SALES. . . .
— FRANCHISE ROYALTIES. . . .
— OTHER. We license our brand for certain foods, clothing, books and other products. We also generate revenues from the publishing of books and magazines and third-party advertising.

The following graph sets forth our revenues by category for the 1996, 1997, 1998, 1999 and 2000 fiscal years.

[Table Omitted: eds.]

— ACCELERATED GROWTH IN CONTINENTAL EUROPE. In Continental Europe, we have accelerated growth by adapting our business model to local conditions, implementing more aggressive marketing programs tailored to the local markets. . . . Attendance in our Continental Europe operations increased by 79% to 7.0 million in 2000 from 3.9 million in fiscal 1997.
— INCREASED PRODUCT SALES. We have increased our product sales by 265% from fiscal 1997 to 2000 by introducing new products and optimizing our product mix. . . .

Our worldwide attendance has grown by 55% in our company-owned operations from 23.0 million in fiscal 1997 to 35.7 million in 2000, and our operating profit margin has grown from 6.7% (before a restructuring charge) in fiscal 1997 to 25.9% in 2000.

ATTENDANCE IN COMPANY-OWNED OPERATIONS
(in millions)

[Table Omitted: eds.]

RESULTS OF OPERATIONS

The following table summarizes our historical income from operations as a percentage of revenues for the fiscal years ended April 25, 1998, April 24, 1999 and April 29, 2000, the eight months ended December 30, 2000 and the nine months ended October 28, 2000 and September 29, 2001.

| | FISCAL YEAR ENDED | | | EIGHT MONTHS ENDED | NINE MONTHS ENDED | |
	APRIL 25, 1998	APRIL 24, 1999	APRIL 29, 2000	DEC. 30, 2000	OCT. 28, 2000	SEPT. 29, 2001
Total revenues, net	100.0%	100.0%	100.0%	100.0%	100.0%	100.0%
Cost of revenues	53.8	49.1	50.4	51.0	48.7	45.0
Gross profit	46.2	50.9	49.6	49.0	51.3	55.0
Marketing expenses	16.6	14.5	12.9	9.9	10.8	10.8
Selling, general and administrative expenses	14.8	13.4	12.7	11.8	11.9	10.8
Operating income	14.8%	23.0%	24.0%	27.3%	28.6%	33.4%

COMPARISON OF THE NINE MONTHS ENDED SEPTEMBER 29, 2001 (39 WEEKS) TO THE NINE MONTHS ENDED OCTOBER 28, 2000 (40 WEEKS).

The nine months ended October 28, 2000, is, in the opinion of management, the available period most comparable to the nine months ended September 29, 2001.

[Five Page Narrative of the Above Omitted: Eds.]

LIQUIDITY AND CAPITAL RESOURCES

During the eight months ended December 30, 2000 and for the nine months ended September 29, 2001, our primary source of funds to meet working capital needs was cash from operations. For the eight months ended December 30, 2000 cash flows provided by operating activities were $28.9 million. Cash and cash equivalents increased $0.5 million to $44.5 million during the eight months ended December 30, 2000. For the eight months ended December 30, 2000, cash flows provided by operating activities of $28.9 million were used primarily to fund a loan of $16.8 million to WeightWatchers.com and to repay principal on our outstanding senior credit facilities of $7.1 million. . . .

We believe that cash flows from operating activities, together with borrowings available under our revolving credit facility, will be sufficient for the next twelve months to fund currently anticipated capital expenditure requirements, debt service requirements and working capital expenditure requirements. Any future acquisitions, joint ventures or other similar transactions will likely require additional capital and we cannot be certain that any additional capital will be available on acceptable terms or at all. . . .

Our senior credit facilities contain covenants that restrict our ability to incur additional indebtedness, pay dividends on and redeem capital stock, make other restricted payments, including investments, sell our assets and enter into consolidations, mergers and transfers of all or substantially all of our assets. Our senior credit facilities also require us to maintain specified financial ratios and satisfy financial condition tests. These tests and financial ratios become more restrictive over the life of the senior credit facilities. . . .

In addition, we have one million shares of Series A Preferred Stock issued and outstanding with a preference value of $25.0 million. Holders of the Series A Preferred Stock are entitled to receive dividends at an annual rate of 6% payable annually in arrears. If there is a liquidation, dissolution or winding up, the holders of shares of Series A Preferred Stock are entitled to be paid out of our assets available for distribution to shareholders an amount in cash equal to the $25 liquidation preference per share plus all accrued and unpaid dividends prior to the distribution of any assets to holders of shares of our common stock. Subject to the restrictions set forth in our debt instruments, holders of our Series A Preferred Stock will have the right to cause us to repurchase their shares upon completion of this offering. If we are required to repurchase the Series A Preferred Stock, we expect that we would finance the purchase with our available cash or borrowings under our revolving credit facility. . . .

SEASONALITY

Our business is seasonal, with revenues generally decreasing at year end and during the summer months. Our advertising schedule supports the three key enrollment-generating seasons of the year: winter, spring and fall. Due to the timing of our marketing expenditures, particularly the higher level of expenditures in the first quarter, our operating income for the second quarter is generally the strongest, with the fourth quarter being the weakest.

The following table summarizes our historical quarterly results of operations for the periods indicated. We believe this presentation illustrates the seasonal nature of our business.

	HISTORICAL QUARTER ENDED						
				TWO MONTHS ENDED			
	APRIL 29, 2000	JULY 29, 2000	OCT. 28, 2000	DEC. 30, 2000	MARCH 31, 2001	JUNE 30, 2001	SEPT. 29, 2001
	(14 weeks)	(13 weeks)	(13 weeks)	(9 weeks) (in millions)	(13 weeks)	(13 weeks)	(13 weeks)
Revenues, net	$132.8	$103.1	$107.6	$62.5	$172.0	$162.3	$144.0
Gross profit	70.0	54.8	51.5	27.6	94.6	90.6	78.0
Marketing expenses	18.6	6.7	11.8	8.5	27.1	13.5	10.9
Selling, general and administrative expenses	17.2	11.5	12.0	8.7	17.7	17.8	16.2
Operating income	34.2	36.6	27.7	10.4	49.8	59.3	50.9
Net income (loss)	17.5	13.7	10.9	(9.6)	23.2	26.1	16.1

As a result of the Weighco acquisition, we believe the following table summarizing our pro forma quarterly results of operations is more indicative of the impact of seasonality on our business than our historical quarterly results of operations.

	PROFORMA QUARTER ENDED			HISTORICAL QUARTER ENDED			
				TWO MONTHS ENDED			
	APRIL 29, 2000	JULY 29, 2000	OCT. 28, 2000	DEC. 30, 2000	MARCH 31, 2001	JUNE 30, 2001	SEPT. 29, 2001
	(14 weeks)	(13 weeks)	(13 weeks)	(9 weeks) (in millions)	(13 weeks)	(13 weeks)	(13 weeks)
Revenues, net	$145.4	$116.1	$120.6	$69.8	$173.8	$162.3	$144.0
Gross profit	77.9	62.1	58.8	319	95.9	90.6	78.0
Marketing expenses	20.1	7.4	12.8	8.8	27.4	13.5	10.9
Selling, general and administrative expenses	20.1	14.3	14.9	10.6	17.9	17.8	16.2
Operating income	37.7	40.4	31.1	12.5	50.6	59.3	50.9
Net income (loss)	18.4	14.5	11.6	(9.2)	23.5	26.1	16.1

Effective April 30, 2000, we changed our fiscal year end from the last Saturday in April to the Saturday closest to December 31. As a result of the change in our reporting period, beginning in 2001, we believe that our first quarter will typically have the highest revenue, followed by the second, third and fourth quarters, respectively.

ACCOUNTING STANDARDS

In July 2001, the Financial Accounting Standards Board issued Statement of Financial Accounting Standards, or SFAS, No. 141, "Business Combinations," and SFAS No. 142, "Goodwill and Other Intangible Assets." SFAS 141 requires that all business combinations initiated after June 30, 2001 be accounted for by the purchase method of accounting. SFAS 142 specifies that goodwill and indefinite-lived intangible assets will no longer be amortized, but instead will be subject to annual impairment testing. We will adopt SFAS 142 on December 30, 2001. We are currently evaluating the effect that implementation of the new standards will have on our financial position, results of operations and cash flows.

QUANTITATIVE AND QUALITATIVE DISCLOSURES ABOUT MARKET RISK

We are exposed to foreign currency fluctuations and interest rate changes. . . .

We enter into forward and swap contracts to hedge transactions denominated in foreign currencies to reduce the currency risk associated with fluctuating exchange rates. These contracts are used primarily to hedge certain intercompany cash flows and for payments arising from some of our foreign currency denominated obligations. Realized and unrealized gains and losses from these transactions are included in net income for the period. . . .

INDUSTRY

OVERVIEW

The number of overweight and obese people worldwide has been increasing due to improving living standards and changing eating patterns, as well as increasingly sedentary lifestyles. The World Health Organization has reported that the world's population is becoming overweight at a rapid pace. According to the organization, in 2000, over one billion people worldwide were overweight and there exists an urgent need to deal with this problem. In the United States, the proportion of U.S. adults who are overweight has increased from 47% to 61% over the last 20 years, and approximately 52 million Americans are currently dieting. . . .

COMPETITION

The weight-loss market includes commercial weight-loss programs, self-help weight-loss products, Internet-based weight-loss products, dietary supplements, weight-loss services administered by doctors, nutritionists and dieticians and weight-loss drugs. Competition among commercial weight-loss programs is largely based on program recognition and reputation and the effectiveness, safety and price of the program. . . .

BUSINESS

OVERVIEW

We are a leading global branded consumer company and the leading provider of weight-loss services in 27 countries around the world. Our programs help people lose weight and maintain their weight loss and, as a result, improve their health, enhance their lifestyles and build self-confidence. At the core of our business are weekly meetings, which promote weight loss through education and group support in conjunction with a flexible, healthy diet. Each week, more than one million members attend approximately 37,000 Weight Watchers meetings, which are run by over 13,000 classroom leaders. Our classroom leaders teach, inspire, motivate and act as role models for our members. . . .

We have experienced strong growth in sales and profits over the last five years since we made the strategic decision to re-focus our meetings exclusively on our group education approach. . . .

The following table sets forth our NACO operations and international attendance for the 1997, 1998, 1999 and 2000 fiscal years and the twelve months ended April 28, 2001. . . .

MARKET OPPORTUNITY

The large and growing global weight-loss market provides us with significant growth potential. In addition, we also believe that we can increase our penetration rate of our target demographic market of overweight women, ages 25 to 64, in our existing major markets as well as in our less developed markets.

The following chart illustrates our level of penetration of our target market . . . [for 13 countries]:

[Table Omitted: eds.]

RELATIVE SIZE OF TARGET MARKET

. . . We have demonstrated the ability to enter new markets as our program has proven adaptable in 27 countries. We customize our program for each geographic setting by tailoring the program for the local language, culture and food preferences. We believe that our international success proves that our core weight-loss program is effective worldwide and have recently begun operations in Spain and Denmark. . . .

OUR BILLION DOLLAR BRAND

WEIGHT WATCHERS is the leading global weight-loss brand with retail sales of over $1.5 billion in 2000, including licensees and franchisees. Currently, over 97% of U.S. women recognize the WEIGHT WATCHERS brand. In addition, our program is the most widely recommended weight-loss program by U.S. doctors. Our credibility is further enhanced by the endorsement of the U.S. Department of Agriculture. . . .

WEIGHT WATCHERS MEETINGS

We present our program in a series of weekly classes of approximately one hour in duration. Classes are conveniently scheduled throughout the day.

Typically, we hold classes in either meeting rooms rented from civic or religious organizations or in leased locations. [Three pages describing standard operating procedures for classes and core elements of the program's philosophy are omitted. eds.]

ADDITIONAL DELIVERY METHODS

We have developed additional delivery methods for people who, either through circumstance or personal preference, do not attend our classes. For example, we have developed program cookbooks and an AT HOME self-help product that provide information on our diet and guidance on weight loss, as well as CD-ROM versions of our diet for the United Kingdom, Continental Europe and Australia.

Our affiliate and licensee, WeightWatchers.com, recently introduced in the United States WEIGHT WATCHERS ONLINE, an online paid subscription product. . . .

PRODUCT SALES

We sell a range of proprietary products, including snack bars, books, CD-ROMS and POINTS calculators, that is consistent with our brand image. We sell our products primarily through our classroom operations and to our franchisees. In 2000, sales of our proprietary products represented 26% of our revenues, up from 11% in fiscal 1997. . . .

FRANCHISE OPERATIONS

We have enjoyed a mutually beneficial relationship with our franchisees over many years. In our early years, we used an aggressive franchising strategy to quickly establish a meeting infrastructure throughout the world to pre-empt competition. After buying back a significant number of our franchisees, our franchised operations represented approximately 35% of our total worldwide attendance for the nine months ended September 29, 2001. . . . Franchisees typically pay us a fee equal to 10% of their meeting fee revenues.

Our franchisees are responsible for operating classes in their territory using the program we have developed. We provide a central support system for the program and our brand. . . . Most franchise agreements are perpetual and can be terminated only upon a material breach or bankruptcy of the franchisee.

We do not intend to award new franchise territories. From time to time we repurchase franchise territories.

LICENSING

As a highly recognized global brand, WEIGHT WATCHERS is a powerful marketing tool for us and for third parties. We currently license the WEIGHT WATCHERS brand in certain categories of food, apparel, books and other products. . . .

During the period that Heinz owned our company, it developed a number of food product lines under the WEIGHT WATCHERS brand, with hundreds of millions of dollars of retail sales, mostly in the United States and in the United Kingdom.

. . . Heinz has retained a perpetual royalty-free license to continue using our brand in its core food categories. . . .

We have begun focusing on proactively developing new licensing opportunities with a number of food companies and have hired a general manager to focus exclusively on this area. . . .

MARKETING AND PROMOTION

MEMBER REFERRALS

An important source of new members is through word-of-mouth generated by our current and former members. . . .

MEDIA ADVERTISING

. . . We allocate our media advertising on a market-by-market basis, as well as by media vehicle (television, radio, magazines and newspapers), taking into account the target market and the effectiveness of the medium.

DIRECT MAIL

Direct mail is a critical element of our marketing because it targets potential returning members. We maintain a database of current and former members, which we use to focus our direct mailings. During 2000 our NACO operations sent over eight million pieces of direct mail. Most of these mailings are timed to coincide with the start of the diet seasons. . . .

PRICING STRUCTURE AND PROMOTIONS

Our most popular payment structure is a "pay-as-you-go" arrangement. Typically, a new member pays an initial registration fee and then a weekly fee for each class attended, although free registration is often offered as a promotion. Our LIBERTY/LOYALTY payment plan provides members with the option of committing to consecutive weekly attendance with a lower weekly fee with penalties for missed classes or paying a higher weekly fee without the missed meeting penalties. We also offer discounted prepayment options.

PUBLIC RELATIONS AND CELEBRITY ENDORSEMENTS

The focus of our public relations efforts is through our current and former members who have successfully lost weight on our program. . . .

For many years we have also used celebrities to promote and endorse the program. . . .

WEIGHT WATCHERS MAGAZINE

WEIGHT WATCHERS MAGAZINE is an important branded marketing channel that is experiencing strong growth. We re-acquired the rights to publish the magazine in February 2000. Since its U.S. re-launch in March 2000, circulation has grown from zero to over 500,000 in September 2001, and the magazine has a readership of over two million. . . .

WEIGHTWATCHERS.COM

Our affiliate and licensee, WeightWatchers.com, operates the WEIGHT WATCHERS website, which is an important global promotional channel for our brand and businesses. The website contributes value to our classroom business by promoting our brand, advertising Weight Watchers classes and keeping members involved with the program outside the classroom through useful offerings, such as a meeting locator, low calorie recipes, weight-loss news articles, success stories and on-line forums. . . .

Under our agreement with WeightWatchers.com, we granted it an exclusive license to use our trademarks, copyrights and domain names on the Internet in connection with its online weight-loss business. The license agreement provides us with control of how our intellectual property is used. In particular, we have the right to approve WeightWatchers.com's e-commerce activities, strategies and operational plans, marketing programs, privacy policy and materials publicly displayed on the Internet.

We own 19.8% of WeightWatchers.com, or 38.1% on a fully diluted basis (including the exercise of all options and all warrants), and beginning in January 2002, we will receive royalties of 10% of WeightWatchers. com's net revenues.

ENTREPRENEURIAL MANAGEMENT

We run our company in a decentralized and entrepreneurial manner that allows us to develop and test new ideas on a local basis and then implement the most successful ideas across our network. . . .

HISTORY

EARLY DEVELOPMENT

In 1961, Jean Nidetch, the founder of our company, attended a New York City obesity clinic and took what she learned from her personal experience at the obesity clinic and began weight-loss meetings with a group of her overweight friends in the basement of a New York apartment building. Under Ms. Nidetch's leadership, the group members supported each other in their weight-loss efforts, and word of the group's success quickly spread. Ms. Nidetch and Al and Felice Lippert, who all successfully lost weight through these efforts, formally launched Weight Watchers.

HEINZ OWNERSHIP

Recognizing the power of the WEIGHT WATCHERS brand, Heinz acquired us in 1978 in large part to acquire the rights to our name for its food business. . . .

ARTAL OWNERSHIP

In September 1999, Artal Luxembourg acquired us from Heinz. . . .

REGULATION AND LITIGATION

A number of laws and regulations govern our advertising, franchise operations and relations with consumers. . . .

During the mid-1990s, the FTC filed complaints against a number of commercial weight-loss providers alleging violations of the Federal Trade Commission Act by the use and content of advertisements for weight-loss programs that featured testimonials, claims for program success and safety and statements as to program costs to participants. In 1997, we entered into a consent order with the FTC settling all contested issues raised in the complaint filed against us. The consent order requires us to comply with certain procedures and disclosures in connection with our advertisements . . . [and] does not contain any admission of guilt nor require us to pay any civil penalties or damages. . . .

We are involved in legal proceedings incidental to our business. Although the outcome of these matters cannot be predicted with certainty, our management believes that none of these matters will have an adverse effect on our financial condition, results of operations or cash flows.

EMPLOYEES AND SERVICE PROVIDERS

As of September 29, 2001, we had approximately 34,000 employees and service providers, of which 13,100 were located in the United States, 13,000 were located in the United Kingdom, 3,300 were located in Continental Europe and 4,600 were located in Australia and New Zealand. . . . None of our service providers or employees is represented by a labor union. We consider our employee relations to be satisfactory.

PROPERTIES

We are headquartered in Woodbury, New York in a leased office. Each of the four NACO regions has a small regional office. The Woodbury, New York lease expires in 2005, the Paramus, New Jersey lease expires in 2007, and the New York, New York WEIGHT WATCHERS MAGAZINE lease expires in 2002. Our other North American office leases are short-term. Our operations in each country also each have one head office.

We typically hold our classes in third-party locations (typically meeting rooms in well-located civic or religious organizations or space leased in shopping centers). . . .

MANAGEMENT

DIRECTORS AND EXECUTIVE OFFICERS

Set forth below are the names, ages as of June 30, 2001 and current positions with us and our subsidiaries of our executive officers and directors.

NAME	AGE	POSITION
Linda Huett	56	President and Chief Executive Officer, Director
Richard McSorley	57	Chief Operating Officer, NACO
Clive Brothers	47	Chief Operating Officer, Europe
Scott R. Penn	30	Vice President, Australasia
Thomas S. Kiritsis	57	Vice President, Chief Financial Officer
Robert W. Hollweg	58	Vice President, General Counsel and Secretary
Raymond Debbane[1][2]	46	Chairman of the Board
Jonas M. Fajgenbaum	29	Director
Sacha Lainovic[1]	44	Director
Christopher J. Sobecki[2]	43	Director

[1]Member of our compensation and benefits committee.

[2]Member of our audit committee.

[Individual Biographies Omitted: eds.]

BOARD OF DIRECTORS

Our board of directors is currently comprised of five directors. We expect our board of directors to consist of nine members within twelve months of this offering. We expect to add two independent members to our board of directors within three months after the consummation of this offering and a third independent member to our board of directors within twelve months after the consummation of this offering.

BOARD OF DIRECTORS REPORT ON EXECUTIVE COMPENSATION PROGRAMS

Our board of directors oversees the compensation programs of our company, with particular attention to the compensation for our Chief Executive Officer and the other executive officers. It is the responsibility of our board of directors to review, recommend and approve changes to our compensation policies and benefits programs, to administer our stock plans, including approving stock option grants to executive officers and other stock option grants, and to otherwise ensure that our compensation philosophy is consistent with the best interests of our company and is properly implemented.

Our compensation philosophy is to (a) provide a competitive total compensation package that enables us to attract and retain key executive and employee talent needed to accomplish our goals and (b) directly link compensation to improvements in our company's financial and operational performance.

Total compensation is comprised of a base salary plus both cash and non-cash incentive compensation, and is based on our financial performance and other factors, and is delivered through a combination of cash and equity-based awards. . . .

Our board of directors believes that granting stock options provides officers with a strong economic interest in maximizing shareholder returns over the longer term. . . .

Our board of directors will continue to monitor our compensation program in order to maintain the proper balance between cash compensation and equity-based incentives and may consider further revisions in the future, although it is expected that equity-based compensation will remain one of the principal components of compensation.

COMMITTEES OF OUR BOARD OF DIRECTORS

The standing committees of our board of directors will consist of an audit committee and a compensation and benefits committee.

AUDIT COMMITTEE

The principal duties of our audit committee are as follows:

— to oversee that our management has maintained the reliability and integrity of our accounting policies and financial reporting and our disclosure practices;
— to oversee that our management has established and maintained processes to assure that an adequate system of internal control is functioning;
— to oversee that our management has established and maintained processes to assure our compliance with all applicable laws, regulations and corporate policy;
— to review our annual and quarterly financial statements prior to their filing or prior to the release of earnings; and
— to review the performance of the independent accountants and make recommendations to the board of directors regarding the appointment or termination of the independent accountants.

The audit committee has the power to investigate any matter brought to its attention within the scope of its duties and to retain counsel for this purpose where appropriate.

We plan to appoint two independent members of the audit committee within three months following this offering and the third independent member within twelve months after the consummation of this offering.

COMPENSATION AND BENEFITS COMMITTEE

The principal duties of the compensation and benefits committee are as follows:

— to review key employee compensation policies, plans and programs;

— to monitor performance and compensation of our employee-director, officers and other key employees;

— to prepare recommendations and periodic reports to the board of directors concerning these matters; and

— to function as the committee which administers the incentive programs referred to in "Executive Compensation" below. . . .

CLASSES AND TERMS OF DIRECTORS

Our board of directors is divided into three classes, as nearly equal in number as possible, with each director serving a three-year term and one class being elected at each year's annual meeting of shareholders. As of the date of this prospectus, the following individuals are directors and will serve for the terms indicated:

Class 1 Directors (term expiring in 2002)
   Raymond Debbane
   Jonas M. Fajgenbaum
Class 2 Directors (term expiring in 2003)
   Sacha Lainovic
   Christopher J. Sobecki
Class 3 Director (term expiring in 2004)
   Linda Huett

EXECUTIVE COMPENSATION

The following table sets forth for the twelve months ended December 30, 2000, and for the fiscal years ended April 29, 2000 and April 24, 1999, the compensation paid to our President and Chief Executive Officer and to each of the next four most highly compensated executive officers whose total annual salary and bonus was in excess of $100,000.

SUMMARY COMPENSATION TABLE

[Table's Data Omitted: eds.]

In December 1999, our board of directors adopted the "1999 Stock Purchase and Option Plan of Weight Watchers International, Inc. and Subsidiaries" under which selected employees were afforded the opportunity to purchase shares of our common stock and/or were granted options to purchase shares of our common stock. The number of shares available for grant under this plan is 7,058,040 shares of our authorized common stock. The following table sets forth information regarding options granted during the twelve months ended December 30, 2000 to the named executive officers under our stock purchase and option plan.

WEIGHT WATCHERS INTERNATIONAL, INC. AND SUBSIDIARIES OPTION GRANTS FOR THE TWELVE MONTHS ENDED DECEMBER 30, 2000

	INDIVIDUAL GRANTS				
NAME	NUMBER OF SECURITIES UNDERLYING OPTIONS GRANTED	PERCENT OF TOTAL OPTIONS GRANTED TO EMPLOYEES IN TWELVE MONTHS ENDED DECEMBER 30, 2000	EXERCISE OR BASE PRICE (PER SHARE)	EXPIRATION DATE	GRANT DATE PRESENT VALUE[3]
Linda Huett	141,161	28.6%	$2.13	July 4, 2010	$138,600
Thomas S. Kiritsis ...	282,322	57.1%	$2.13	June 14, 2010	$279,000

[3] The estimated grant date's present value is determined using the Black-Scholes model. The adjustments and assumptions incorporated in the Black-Scholes model in estimating the value of the grants include the following: (a) the exercise price of the options equals the fair market value of the underlying stock on the date of grant; (b) an option term of 10 years; (c) dividend yield and volatility of 0%; and (d) a risk free interest rate ranging from 6.20% to 6.26%. The ultimate value, if any, an optionee will realize upon exercise of an option will depend on the excess of the market value of our common stock over the exercise price of the option.

Under our 1999 Stock Purchase and Option Plan, we have the ability to grant stock options, restricted stock, stock appreciation rights and other stock-based awards. Generally, stock options granted under this plan vest and become exercisable in annual increments over five years with respect to one-third of options granted, and the remaining two-thirds of the options vest on the ninth anniversary of the date the options were granted, subject to accelerated vesting upon our achievement of certain performance targets. In any event, the options that vest over five years automatically become fully vested upon the occurrence of a change in control of our company.

[Various Tables Regarding Options and Stock Appreciation Rights Outstanding Omitted: eds.]

RELATED PARTY TRANSACTIONS

THE SUMMARIES OF THE AGREEMENTS DESCRIBED BELOW ARE NOT COMPLETE. YOU SHOULD READ THE AGREEMENTS IN THEIR ENTIRETY, WHICH HAVE BEEN FILED WITH THE SEC

AS EXHIBITS TO THE REGISTRATION STATEMENT OF WHICH THIS PROSPECTUS IS A PART.

SHAREHOLDERS' AGREEMENTS

Simultaneously with the closing of our acquisition by Artal Luxembourg, we entered into a shareholders' agreement with Artal Luxembourg and Heinz that governs our relationship surrounding our common stock. Subsequent transferees of Artal Luxembourg and Heinz must, subject to limited exceptions, agree to be bound by the terms and provisions of the agreement. Heinz has sold all shares of our common stock held by it and accordingly no longer has any rights or obligations under this agreement. We and Artal Luxembourg recently terminated this agreement.

Shortly after our acquisition by Artal Luxembourg, we entered into a shareholders' agreement with Artal Luxembourg and Merchant Capital, Inc., Richard and Heather Penn, Longisland International Limited, Envoy Partners and Scotiabanc, Inc. that governs our relationship surrounding our common stock held by these parties other than Artal Luxembourg. Without the consent of Artal Luxembourg, transfers of our common stock by these shareholders are restricted with certain exceptions. . . .

REGISTRATION RIGHTS AGREEMENT

Simultaneously with the closing of our acquisition by Artal Luxembourg, we entered into a registration rights agreement with Artal Luxembourg and Heinz. The registration rights agreement grants Artal Luxembourg the right to require us to register its shares of our common stock for public sale under the Securities Act (1) upon demand and (2) in the event that we conduct certain types of registered offerings. . . .

PREFERRED SHAREHOLDERS' AGREEMENT

Simultaneously with the closing of our acquisition by Artal Luxembourg, we entered into a preferred shareholders' agreement with Heinz that governs our relationship concerning our Series A Preferred Stock. Subsequent transferees of Heinz, subject to limited exceptions, must agree to be bound by the terms and provisions of this agreement. Artal Luxembourg and we have a preemptive right to acquire the preferred stock from Heinz if Heinz receives an offer to purchase any or all of its preferred stock from a third party and it wishes to accept the offer. As a result of this offering, Heinz has the right to require us to redeem limited by the provisions contained in our credit agreement and the indentures pursuant to which our senior subordinated notes were issued. . . .

LIMITED LIABILITY COMPANY AGREEMENT

Simultaneously with the closing of our acquisition by Artal Luxembourg, we contributed $2,500 in exchange for a 50% membership interest in

WW Foods, LLC, a Delaware limited liability company. Heinz owns the remaining 50% interest. The purpose of WW Foods is to own, maintain and preserve WEIGHT WATCHERS food and beverage trademarks that were contributed to it by Heinz. WW Foods serves as the vehicle for licensing rights in those food and beverage trademarks to us and to Heinz, and for the licensing of program information by our company to Heinz.

LICENSING AGREEMENTS

The licensing agreements govern the ownership and rights to use the WEIGHT WATCHERS and other trademarks, service marks and related rights among our company, Heinz and WW Foods. As described below, the licensing agreements address the parties' respective ownership and rights to use food and beverage trademarks, service marks, program standards, program information, program information trademarks and third party licenses. Heinz is also a party to the operating agreement, which helps preserve and enhance these trademarks, service marks and related rights and facilitates their orderly use by each party.

FOOD AND BEVERAGE TRADEMARKS

Under the licensing agreements, we distributed to Heinz and Heinz contributed to WW Foods all WEIGHT WATCHERS trademarks and other trademarks we owned relating to food and beverage products. However, Heinz retained certain trademarks previously used by Heinz in connection with those food and beverage trademarks that do not include the WEIGHT WATCHERS name (including, for example, SMART ONES), which we distributed to Heinz. At the closing of our acquisition by Artal Luxembourg, WW Foods granted an exclusive, worldwide, royalty-free, perpetual license to use the food and beverage trademarks:

— to Heinz, for worldwide use on food products in specified product categories . . . ; and
— to us, for use on all other food and beverage products. . . .

At the closing of our acquisition by Artal Luxembourg, we granted to Heinz an exclusive, worldwide, royalty-free license to use those food and beverage trademarks (or any portion covering food and beverage products) that we hold in custody for the benefit of WW Foods in connection with the other products licensed to Heinz by WW Foods. . . .

PROGRAM STANDARDS

We have exclusive control of the dietary principles to be followed in any eating or lifestyle regimen to facilitate weight loss or weight control employed by the classroom business such as WINNING POINTS. Except for specified limitations concerning products currently sold and

39

extensions of existing product lines, Heinz may use the food and beverage related trademarks only on Heinz licensed products that have been specially formulated to be compatible with our dietary principles. We have exclusive responsibility for enforcing compliance with our dietary principles. . . .

THIRD PARTY LICENSES

Under the licensing agreements, we assigned to Heinz all licenses that we previously granted to third parties, and Heinz retained all existing sub-licenses granted by it to third parties under a license previously granted to Heinz, that relate to the manufacture, distribution or sale of food and beverage products.

MANAGEMENT AGREEMENT

Simultaneously with the closing of our acquisition by Artal Luxembourg, we entered into a management agreement with The Invus Group, Ltd., the independent investment advisor to Artal Luxembourg. Under this agreement, The Invus Group provides us with management, consulting and other services in exchange for an annual fee equal to the greater of one million dollars or one percent of our EBITDA (as defined in the indentures relating to our senior subordinated notes), plus any related out-of-pocket expenses. This agreement is terminable at the option of The Invus Group at any time or by us at any time after Artal Luxembourg owns less than a majority of our voting stock.

CORPORATE AGREEMENT

We have entered into a corporate agreement with Artal Luxembourg. We have agreed that, so long as Artal Luxembourg beneficially owns 10% or more, but less than a majority of our then outstanding voting stock, Artal Luxembourg will have the right to nominate a number of directors approximately equal to that percentage multiplied by the number of directors on our board. This right to nominate directors will not restrict Artal Luxembourg from nominating a greater number of directors.

We have agreed with Artal Luxembourg that both Weight Watchers and Artal Luxembourg have the right to:

— engage in the same or similar business activities as the other party;
— do business with any customer or client of the other party; and
— employ or engage any officer or employee of the other party.

Neither Artal Luxembourg nor we, nor our respective related parties, will be liable to each other as a result of engaging in any of these activities.

Under the corporate agreement, if one of our officers or directors who also serves as an officer, director or advisor of Artal Luxembourg becomes aware of a potential transaction related primarily to the group education-based weight-loss business that may represent a corporate opportunity for both Artal Luxembourg and us, the officer, director or advisor has no duty to present that opportunity to Artal Luxembourg, and we will have the sole right to pursue the transaction if our board so determines. If one of our officers or directors who also serves as an officer, director or advisor of Artal Luxembourg becomes aware of any other potential transaction that may represent a corporate opportunity for both Artal Luxembourg and us, the officer or director will have a duty to present that opportunity to Artal Luxembourg, and Artal Luxembourg will have the sole right to pursue the transaction if Artal Luxembourg's board so determines. If one of our officers or directors who does not serve as an officer, director or advisor of Artal Luxembourg becomes aware of a potential transaction that may represent a corporate opportunity for both Artal Luxembourg and us, neither the officer nor the director nor we have a duty to present that opportunity to Artal Luxembourg, and we may pursue the transaction if our board so determines. . . .

WEIGHTWATCHERS.COM NOTE

On September 10, 2001, we amended and restated our loan agreement with WeightWatchers.com, increasing the aggregate commitment thereunder to $34.5 million. The principal amount may be advanced at any time or from time to time prior to July 31, 2003. The note bears interest at 13% per year, beginning on January 1, 2002, which interest, except as set forth below, shall be paid semi-annually starting on March 31, 2002. All principal outstanding under this note will be payable in six semi-annual installments, starting on March 31, 2004. . . .

WEIGHTWATCHERS.COM WARRANT AGREEMENTS

Under the warrant agreements that we entered with WeightWatchers. com, we have received warrants to purchase an additional 6,394,997 shares of WeightWatchers.com's common stock in connection with the loans that we made to WeightWatchers.com under the note described above. These warrants will expire from November 24, 2009 to September 10, 2011 and may be exercised at a price of $7.14 per share of Weight-Watchers.com's common stock until their expiration. We own 19.8% of the outstanding common stock of WeightWatchers.com, or 38.1% on a fully diluted basis (including the exercise of all options and all the warrants we own in WeightWatchers.com).

COLLATERAL ASSIGNMENT AND SECURITY AGREEMENT

In connection with the WeightWatchers.com note, we entered into a collateral assignment and security agreement whereby we obtained a security interest in the assets of WeightWatchers.com. Our security interest in those assets will terminate when the note has been paid in full.

WEIGHTWATCHERS.COM INTELLECTUAL PROPERTY LICENSE

We have entered into an amended and restated intellectual property license agreement with WeightWatchers.com that governs WeightWatchers.com's right to use our trademarks and materials related to the Weight Watchers program. . . .

Beginning in January 2002, WeightWatchers.com will pay us a royalty of 10% of the net revenues it earns through its online activities.

We retain exclusive ownership of all of the trademarks and materials that we license to WeightWatchers.com and of the derivative works created by WeightWatchers.com. . . .

The license agreement provides us with control over the use of our intellectual property. We will have the right to approve any e-commerce activities, any materials, sublicense, communication to consumers, products, privacy policy, strategies, marketing and operational plans Weight-Watchers.com intends to use or implement in connection with its online weight-loss business. . . .

WEIGHTWATCHERS.COM REGISTRATION RIGHTS AGREEMENT

We entered into a registration rights agreement with WeightWatchers.com, Artal Luxembourg and Heinz with respect to our shares in WeightWatchers.com. Heinz has resold all of its shares in WeightWatchers.com back to WeightWatchers.com and thus no longer has any rights under this agreement. The registration rights agreement grants Artal Luxembourg the right to require WeightWatchers.com to register its shares of Weight-Watchers.com common stock upon demand and also grants us and Artal Luxembourg rights to register and sell shares of WeightWatchers.com's common stock in the event it conducts certain types of registered offerings.

WEIGHTWATCHERS.COM LEASE GUARANTEE

We have guaranteed the performance of WeightWatcher.com's lease of its office space at 888 Seventh Avenue, New York, New York. The annual rental rate is $459,000 plus increases for operating expenses and real estate taxes. The lease expires in September 2003.

NELLSON CO-PACK AGREEMENT

We entered into an agreement with Nellson Nutraceutical, a subsidiary of Artal Luxembourg, to purchase snack bar and powder products manufactured by Nellson Nutraceutical for sale at our meetings. . . . We purchased $4.9 million and $4.3 million, respectively, of products from Nellson Nutraceutical during the eight months ended December 30, 2000 and the twelve months ended April 29, 2000. The term of the agreement runs through December 31, 2004, and we have the option to renew the agreement for successive one-year periods by providing written notice to Nellson Nutraceutical.

PRINCIPAL AND SELLING SHAREHOLDERS

The following table sets forth information regarding the beneficial ownership of our common stock by (1) all persons known by us to own beneficially more than 5% of our common stock, (2) our chief executive officer and
each of the named executive officers, (3) each director, (4) all directors and
executive officers as a group and (5) each selling shareholder.

Beneficial ownership is determined in accordance with the rules of
the Securities and Exchange Commission. . . .

Our capital stock consists of our common stock and our preferred
stock. As of September 29, 2001, there were 105,407,142 shares of our
common stock and 1,000,000 shares of our preferred stock outstanding.

NAME OF BENEFICIAL OWNER	AS OF SEPTEMBER 29, 2001 SHARES	PERCENT	SHARES TO BE SOLD IN OFFERING	IMMEDIATELY AFTER THIS OFFERING SHARES	PERCENT
Artal Luxembourg S.A	99,109,939	94.0%	16,047,516	83,062,423	78.8%
Linda Huett	199,979	*	—	199,978	*
Richard McSorley	94,108	*	—	94,108	*
Clive Brothers	164,688	*	—	164,688	*
Scott R. Penn	299,968	*	—	299,967	*
Thomas S. Kiritsis	164,689	*	—	164,688	*
Robert W. Hollweg	188,215	*	—	188,215	*
Raymond Debbane	—	—	—	—	—
Sacha Lainovic	—	—	—	—	—
Christopher J. Sobecki	—	—	—	—	—
Jonas M. Fajgenbaum	—	—	—	—	—
All directors and executive officers as a group (10 people)	1,111,644	1.1%	—	1,111,644	1.1%
Richard and Heather Penn	1,246,921	1.2%	941,072	305,849	*
Merchant Capital, Inc.	941,072	*	152,375	788,697	*
Scotiabanc, Inc.	941,072	*	152,375	788,697	*
Longisland International Limited	658,751	*	106,662	552,089	*

*Less than 1.0%.

[Notes to Schedule Omitted: Eds.]

In addition, certain of the selling shareholders have granted the
underwriters the right to purchase up to an additional 2,610,000 shares of
common stock to cover over-allotments. If the underwriters exercise this
over-allotment option in full, Artal Luxembourg will beneficially own
76.4% of our common stock after this offering.

DESCRIPTION OF INDEBTEDNESS

The following are summaries of the material terms and conditions of our principal indebtedness.

SENIOR CREDIT FACILITIES

. . .

SENIOR SUBORDINATED NOTES

. . .

DESCRIPTION OF CAPITAL STOCK

Our authorized capital stock consists of (1) 1.0 billion shares of common stock, no par value, of which 105,407,142 million shares are issued and outstanding and (2) 250,000,000 shares of preferred stock, no par value, of which 1,000,000 shares are issued and outstanding. As of September 29, 2001, there were 52 holders of our common stock. . . .

The following summary describes elements of our articles of incorporation and bylaws after giving effect to the offering.

COMMON STOCK

VOTING RIGHTS. The holders of our common stock are entitled to one vote per share on all matters submitted for action by the shareholders. There is no provision for cumulative voting with respect to the election of directors. Accordingly, a holder of more than 50% of the shares of our common stock can, if it so chooses, elect all of our directors. In that event, the holders of the remaining shares will not be able to elect any directors.

DIVIDEND RIGHTS. All shares of our common stock are entitled to share equally in any dividends our board of directors may declare from legally available sources. Our senior credit facilities and indentures impose restrictions on our ability to declare dividends with respect to our common stock.

LIQUIDATION RIGHTS. Upon liquidation or dissolution of our company, whether voluntary or involuntary, all shares of our common stock are entitled to share equally in the assets available for distribution to shareholders after payment of all of our prior obligations, including our preferred stock.

OTHER MATTERS. The holders of our common stock have no preemptive or conversion rights and our common stock is not subject to further calls or assessments by us. There are no redemption or sinking fund provisions applicable to the common stock. All outstanding shares of our common stock, including the common stock offered in this offering, are fully paid and non-assessable.

PREFERRED STOCK

We have one million shares of Series A Preferred Stock issued and outstanding. Holders of our Series A Preferred Stock are entitled to receive
dividends at an annual rate of 6% payable annually in arrears. The liquidation preference of our Series A Preferred Stock is $25 per share. In the
event of a liquidation, dissolution or winding up of our company, the
holders of shares of our Series A Preferred Stock will be entitled to be
paid out of our assets available for distribution to our shareholders an
amount in cash equal to the $25 liquidation preference per share plus all
accrued and unpaid dividends prior to the distribution of any assets to
holders of shares of our common stock.

Except as required by law, the holders of our preferred stock have no
voting rights with respect to their shares of preferred stock other than that
the approval of holders of a majority of the outstanding shares of our
preferred stock, voting as a class, will be required to amend, repeal or
change any of the provisions of our articles of incorporation in any
manner that would alter or change the powers, preferences or special
rights of our preferred stock in a way that would affect them adversely.
Without the consent of each holder of the Series A Preferred Stock, no
amendment may reduce the dividend payable on or the liquidation value
of the Series A Preferred Stock.

We may redeem the Series A Preferred Stock, in whole or in part, at
any time or from time to time, at our option, at a price per share equal to
100% of the liquidation value of the preferred stock plus all accrued and
unpaid dividends. . . .

Our board of directors also has the authority, without any further
vote or action by the shareholders, to designate and issue preferred stock
in one or more additional series and to designate the rights, preferences
and privileges of each series, which may be greater than the rights of the
common stock. It is not possible to state the actual effect of the issuance of
any additional series of preferred stock upon the rights of holders of the
common stock until the board of directors determines the specific rights
of the holders of that series. However, the effects might include, among
other things:

— restricting dividends on the common stock;
— diluting the voting power of the common stock;
— impairing the liquidation rights of the common stock; or
— delaying or preventing a change in control without further action
   by the shareholders.

OPTIONS

As of September 29, 2001, there were outstanding 5,763,692 shares of our
common stock issuable upon exercise of outstanding stock options and

1,294,348 shares of our common stock reserved for future issuance under our existing stock option plan.

AUTHORIZED BUT UNISSUED CAPITAL STOCK

The listing requirements of the New York Stock Exchange, which would apply so long as the common stock remains listed on the New York Stock Exchange, require shareholder approval of certain issuances equal to or exceeding 20% of then-outstanding voting power or then-outstanding number of shares of common stock. These additional shares may be used for a variety of corporate purposes, including future public offerings, to raise additional capital or to facilitate acquisitions.

One of the effects of the existence of unissued and unreserved common stock or preferred stock may be to enable our board of directors to issue shares to persons friendly to current management, which issuance could render more difficult or discourage an attempt to obtain control of our company by means of a merger, tender offer, proxy contest or otherwise, and thereby protect the continuity of our management and possibly deprive the shareholders of opportunities to sell their shares of common stock at prices higher than prevailing market prices.

CERTAIN PROVISIONS OF VIRGINIA LAW AND OUR CHARTER AND BYLAWS

Some provisions of Virginia law and our articles of incorporation and bylaws could make the following more difficult:

— acquisition of us by means of a tender offer;
— acquisition of us by means of a proxy contest or otherwise; or
— removal of our incumbent officers and directors.

These provisions, summarized below, are intended to discourage coercive takeover practices and inadequate takeover bids. These provisions are also designed to encourage persons seeking to acquire control of us to first negotiate with our board. We believe that the benefits of increased protection give us the potential ability to negotiate with the proponent of an unfriendly or unsolicited proposal to acquire or restructure us and outweigh the disadvantages of discouraging these proposals because negotiation of these proposals could result in an improvement of their terms.

ELECTION AND REMOVAL OF DIRECTORS

Our board of directors is divided into three classes. . . . This system of electing and removing directors may discourage a third party from making a tender offer or otherwise attempting to obtain control of us because it generally makes it more difficult for shareholders to replace a majority of our directors.

Our articles of incorporation and bylaws do not provide for cumulative voting in the election of directors.

BOARD MEETINGS

Our bylaws provide that the chairman of the board or any two of our directors may call special meetings of the board of directors.

SHAREHOLDER MEETINGS

Our articles of incorporation provide that special meetings of shareholders may be called by the chairman of our board of directors or our president or by a resolution adopted by our board of directors. In addition, our articles of incorporation provide that Artal Luxembourg and certain of its transferees have the right to call special meetings of shareholders prior to the date it ceases to beneficially own 20% of our then-outstanding common stock.

REQUIREMENTS FOR ADVANCE NOTIFICATION OF SHAREHOLDER NOMINATIONS AND PROPOSALS

Our bylaws establish advance notice procedures with respect to shareholder proposals and the nomination of candidates for election as directors, other than nominations made by or at the direction of our board of directors or a committee of the board of directors or by Artal Luxembourg and certain of its transferees when nominating its director designees. In addition, our bylaws provide that so long as Artal Luxembourg or certain of its transferees beneficially owns a majority of our then-outstanding common stock, the foregoing advance notice procedures for shareholder proposals will not apply to it.

SHAREHOLDER ACTION BY WRITTEN CONSENT

Virginia law generally requires shareholder action to be taken only at a meeting of shareholders and permits shareholders to act only by written consent with the unanimous written consent of all shareholders.

AMENDMENT OF ARTICLES OF INCORPORATION AND BYLAW PROVISIONS

Amendment of the provisions described above in our articles of incorporation generally will require an affirmative vote of our directors, as well as the affirmative vote of at least 80% of our then-outstanding voting stock, except that at any time that Artal Luxembourg or certain of its transferees beneficially owns a majority of our then-outstanding common stock, the anti-takeover provisions of our articles of incorporation may be amended by the affirmative vote of a majority of our then-outstanding voting stock. . . .

RIGHTS AGREEMENT

We intend to adopt, prior to consummation of this offering, a rights agreement, subject to the approval of our board. Under the rights agreement, one right will be issued and attached to each share of our common stock including eleven shares that are outstanding. Each right will entitle the holder, in the circumstances described below, to purchase from our company a unit consisting of one one-hundredth of a share of Series B junior participating preferred stock, no par value per share, at an exercise price of $_____ per right, subject to adjustment in certain events. [Five-Page Description of Rights Provision Omitted: Eds.]

LIABILITY OF OFFICERS AND DIRECTORS

Our articles of incorporation require us to indemnify any director, officer or employee who was or is a party to any claim, action or proceeding by reason of his being or having been a director, officer or employee of our company or any other corporation, entity or plan while serving at our request, unless he or she engaged in willful misconduct or a knowing violation of law. Insofar as indemnification for liabilities arising under the Securities Act of 1933 may be permitted to directors, officers or persons controlling us pursuant to the foregoing provisions, we have been informed that, in the opinion of the SEC, indemnification for liabilities under the Securities Act is against public policy and is unenforceable.

ANTI-TAKEOVER STATUTES

We have opted out of the Virginia anti-takeover law regulating "control share acquisitions." . . .

REGISTRAR AND TRANSFER AGENT

The registrar and transfer agent for the common stock is EquiServe Trust Company, N.A.

LISTING

Our common stock has been authorized for listing on the New York Stock Exchange under the symbol "WTW."

SHARES ELIGIBLE FOR FUTURE SALE

Prior to this offering, there has not been any public market for our common stock, and we cannot predict what effect, if any, market sales of shares of common stock or the availability of shares of common stock for sale will have on the market price of our common stock. Nevertheless, sales of substantial amounts of common stock, including shares issued upon the exercise of outstanding options, in the public market, or the perception that these sales could occur, could materially and adversely affect the market price of our common stock and could impair our future ability to raise capital through the sale of our equity or equity-related securities at a time and price that we deem appropriate.

Upon the closing of this offering, we will have outstanding an aggregate of 105,407,142 shares of common stock. Of the outstanding shares, the shares sold in this offering will be freely tradable without restriction or further registration under the Securities Act, except that any shares held by our "affiliates," as that term is defined under Rule 144 of the Securities Act, may be sold only in compliance with the limitations described below. The remaining shares of common stock will be deemed "restricted securities" as defined under Rule 144. Restricted securities may be sold in the public market only if registered or if they qualify for an exemption from registration under Rule 144 or 144(k) under the Securities Act, which we summarize below.

Subject to the lock-up agreements described below, the employee shareholders agreements and the provisions of Rules 144 and 144(k), additional shares of our common stock will be available for sale in the public market under exemptions from registration requirements as follows:

NUMBER OF SHARES	DATE
87,889,507	After 180 days from the date of this prospectus
117,635	At various times after 180 days from the date of this prospectus

Artal Luxembourg, which will own 78.8% of our shares (or 76.4% if the underwriters exercise their over-allotment option in full) upon the closing of this offering, has the ability to cause us to register the resale of its shares.

RULE 144

[Summary of Rule 144 Omitted: Eds.]

LOCK-UP AGREEMENTS

We have agreed that we will not offer, sell, contract to sell, pledge or otherwise dispose of, directly or indirectly, or file with the SEC a registration statement under the Securities Act relating to, any shares of our common stock or securities convertible into or exchangeable or exercisable for any shares of our common stock, or publicly disclose the intention to make any offer, sale, pledge, disposition or filing, without the prior written consent of Credit Suisse First Boston Corporation for a period of 180 days after the date of this prospectus. . . .

Our executive officers and directors and the selling shareholders have [also agreed to a lockup]. . . .

Following this offering, we intend to file a registration statement on Form S-8 under the Securities Act with respect to up to 7,058,040 shares of our common stock that are reserved for issuance pursuant to our stock option plan. . . . However, shares received by employees upon exercise of their options will be subject to certain lock-up agreements. . . .

CERTAIN U.S. FEDERAL INCOME TAX CONSEQUENCES

The following summary describes the material U.S. federal income tax consequences as of the date hereof of the purchase, ownership and disposition of our common stock by a Non-U.S. Holder (as defined below) who holds our common stock as a capital asset. . . . YOU SHOULD CONSULT YOUR OWN TAX ADVISOR CONCERNING THE PARTICULAR U.S. INCOME TAX CONSEQUENCES TO YOU OF THE OWNERSHIP OF THE COMMON STOCK, AS WELL AS THE CONSEQUENCES TO YOU ARISING UNDER THE LAWS OF ANY OTHER TAXING JURISDICTION.

NON-U.S. HOLDERS

. . .

TAXATION OF THE COMMON STOCK

DIVIDENDS. Distributions on our common stock will constitute dividends for United States federal income tax purposes to the extent of our current or accumulated earnings and profits as determined under U.S. federal income tax principles. In general, distributions paid to you will be subject to withholding U.S. federal income tax at a 30% rate or such lower rate as may be specified by an applicable income tax treaty. If you wish to claim the benefit of an applicable treaty rate (and avoid backup withholding as discussed below under "Information Reporting and Backup Withholding"), you will be required to satisfy applicable certification and other requirements. . . .

GAIN ON DISPOSITION OF COMMON STOCK. You generally will not be subject to U.S. federal income tax with respect to gain recognized on a sale or other disposition of common stock unless (i) the gain is effectively connected with your trade or business in the United States, and, where a tax treaty applies, is attributable to a U.S. permanent establishment, (ii) you are an individual and you are present in the United States for 183 or more days in the taxable year of the sale or other disposition and certain other conditions are met, or (iii) you hold (or held at any time within the shorter of the five-year period preceding the sale or other disposition or the period you held our common stock) more than 5% of our common stock and we are or have been at any such time a U.S. real property holding corporation for U.S. federal income tax purposes. . . .

UNDERWRITING

Under the terms and subject to the conditions contained in an underwriting agreement dated _____, 2001, the selling shareholders have agreed to sell to the underwriters named below, for whom Credit Suisse First Boston Corporation and Goldman, Sachs & Co. are acting as representatives, the following respective numbers of shares of common stock:

UNDERWRITER	NUMBER OF SHARES
Credit Suisse First Boston Corporation	
Goldman, Sachs & Co.	
Merrill Lynch, Pierce, Fenner & Smith Incorporated	
Salomon Smith Barney Inc.	
UBS Warburg LLC	
Total	17,400,000

The underwriting agreement provides that the underwriters are obligated to purchase all the shares of common stock in the offering if any are purchased, other than those shares covered by the over-allotment option described below. The underwriting agreement also provides that, if an underwriter defaults, the purchase commitments of non-defaulting underwriters may be increased or the offering may be terminated.

Certain of the selling shareholders have granted to the underwriters a 30-day option to purchase on a pro rata basis up to an aggregate of 2,610,000 additional shares at the initial public offering price less the underwriting discounts and commissions. The option may be exercised only to cover any over-allotments of common stock.

The underwriters propose to offer the shares of common stock initially at the public offering price on the cover page of this prospectus and to selling group members at that price less a selling concession of $_____ per share. The underwriters and selling group members may allow a discount of $_____ per share on sales to other broker/dealers. After the initial public offering the representatives may change the public offering price and concession and discount to broker/dealers.

The following table summarizes the compensation the selling shareholders will pay and the estimated expenses we will pay:

	PER SHARE		TOTAL	
	WITHOUT OVER-ALLOTMENT	WITH OVER-ALLOTMENT	WITHOUT OVER-ALLOTMENT	WITH OVER-ALLOTMENT
Underwriting discounts and commissions paid by selling shareholders...	$	$	$	$
Expenses payable by us	$	$	$	$

51

The representatives have informed us that the underwriters do not expect discretionary sales to exceed 5% of the shares of common stock being offered.

We and the selling shareholders have agreed to indemnify the underwriters against liabilities under the Securities Act, or to contribute to payments which the underwriters may be required to make in that respect.

Prior to this offering, there has been no public market for our common stock. The initial public offering price will be determined by negotiation between the selling shareholders and the representatives and will not necessarily reflect the market price of the common stock following the offering. The principal factors that will be considered in determining the public offering price will include:

— the information in this prospectus and otherwise available to the underwriters;
— market conditions for initial public offerings;
— the history and the prospects for the industry in which we compete;
— the ability of our management;
— the prospects for our future earnings;
— the present state of our development and our current financial condition;
— recent market prices of, and the demand for, publicly traded common stock of generally comparable companies; and
— the general condition of the securities markets at the time of this offering.

We offer no assurances that the initial public offering price will correspond to the price at which the common stock will trade in the public market subsequent to the offering or that an active trading market for the common stock will develop and continue after the offering.

Our common stock has been authorized for listing on the New York Stock Exchange under the symbol "WTW."

In connection with the offering, the underwriters may engage in stabilizing transactions, over-allotment transactions, syndicate covering transactions and penalty bids in accordance with Regulation M under the Securities Exchange Act of 1934.

— Stabilizing transactions permit bids to purchase the underlying security so long as the stabilizing bids do not exceed a specified maximum.
— Over-allotment involves sales by the underwriters of shares in excess of the number of shares the underwriters are obligated to purchase, which creates a syndicate short position. . . .

— Penalty bids permit the representatives to reclaim a selling concession from a syndicate member when the common stock originally sold by the syndicate member is purchased in a stabilizing or syndicate covering transaction to cover syndicate short positions.

These stabilizing transactions . . . and penalty bids may have the effect of raising or maintaining the market price of our common stock or preventing or retarding a decline in the market price of the common stock. As a result, the price of our common stock may be higher than the price that might otherwise exist in the open market. . . .

Some of the underwriters and their affiliates have provided, and may provide in the future, investment banking and other financial services for us in the ordinary course of business for which they have received and would receive customary compensation. Credit Suisse First Boston, New York branch, an affiliate of Credit Suisse First Boston Corporation, is an agent and a lender under our senior credit facilities, and Credit Suisse First Boston Corporation was one of the joint book-running managers for, and an initial purchaser of, our 13% senior subordinated notes due 2009. In addition, Credit Suisse First Boston, New York branch, was a joint lead arranger and joint book manager for our $50 million increase to our senior credit facilities.

Credit Suisse First Boston Corporation also served as financial advisor to Artal Luxembourg in its acquisition of us. The decision of Credit Suisse First Boston Corporation to underwrite our common stock offered hereby was made independent of Credit Suisse First Boston, New York branch, which had no involvement in determining whether to underwrite our common stock under this offering or the terms of this offering. . . .

LEGAL MATTERS

The validity of the issuance of the shares of common stock to be sold in the offering will be passed upon for us by our special Virginia counsel, Hunton & Williams, Richmond, Virginia. Certain legal matters in connection with the issuance of the common stock to be sold in the offering will be passed upon for us by Simpson Thacher & Bartlett, New York, New York. The underwriters have been represented by Cravath, Swaine & Moore, New York, New York.

EXPERTS

The financial statements as of December 30, 2000, April 29, 2000 and April 24, 1999 and for each of the fiscal years ended April 29, 2000, April 24, 1999 and April 25, 1998, the eight months ended December 30, 2000 and the year ended December 30, 2000 included in this prospectus have been so included in reliance on the report of Pricewaterhouse Coopers LLP, independent accountants, given on the authority of said firm as experts in auditing and accounting.

WHERE YOU CAN FIND ADDITIONAL INFORMATION

We file annual, quarterly and current reports and other information with the SEC. You may access and read our SEC filings, including the complete registration statement and all of the exhibits to it, through the SEC's Internet site at www.sec.gov. . . .

We have filed with the SEC a registration statement under the Securities Act with respect to the common stock offered by this prospectus. This prospectus, which constitutes part of the registration statement, does not contain all of the information presented in the registration statement and its exhibits and schedules. Our descriptions in this prospectus of the provisions of documents filed as exhibits to the registration statement or otherwise filed with the SEC are only summaries of the terms of those documents that we consider material. If you want a complete description of the content of the documents, you should obtain the documents yourself by following the procedures described above.

You may request copies of the filings, at no cost, by telephone at (516) 390-1400 or by mail at: 175 Crossways Park West, Woodbury, New York 11797-2055, Attention: Secretary.

INDEX TO FINANCIAL STATEMENTS

F-1

REPORT OF INDEPENDENT ACCOUNTANTS

To the Board of Directors of Weight Watchers International, Inc.:

In our opinion, the accompanying consolidated balance sheets and the related consolidated statements of operations, of cash flows and of changes in shareholders' deficit, parent company investment and comprehensive income present fairly, in all material respects, the consolidated financial position of Weight Watchers International, Inc. and its subsidiaries at December 30, 2000, April 29, 2000 and April 24, 1999, and the results of their operations and their cash flows for the eight months ended December 30, 2000 and for each of the three years in the period ended April 29, 2000, in conformity with accounting principles generally accepted in the United States of America. These financial statements are the responsibility of the Company's management; our responsibility is to express an opinion on these financial statements based on our audits. We conducted our audits of these statements in accordance with auditing standards generally accepted in the United States of America, which require that we plan and perform the audit to obtain reasonable assurance about whether the financial statements are free of material misstatement. An audit includes examining, on a test basis, evidence supporting the amounts and disclo- sures in the financial statements, assessing the accounting principles used and significant estimates made by management, and evaluating the over-all financial statement presentation. We believe that our audits provide a reasonable basis for our opinion.

PricewaterhouseCoopers LLP

New York, New York

[All Financial Statements Omitted: Eds.]

PART II
INFORMATION NOT REQUIRED IN PROSPECTUS

ITEM 13.   OTHER EXPENSES OF ISSUANCE AND DISTRIBUTION.

The actual and estimated expenses in connection with the offering, all of which will be borne by Weight Watchers International, Inc. are as follows:

SEC Registration Fee	$ 115,058
Printing and Engraving Expenses	275,000
Legal Fees	1,000,000
Accounting Fees	500,000
NYSE Listing Fees	250,000
NASD Filing Fee	30,500
Miscellaneous	50,000
Total	$2,220,558

ITEM 14.   INDEMNIFICATION OF DIRECTORS AND OFFICERS.

Our articles of incorporation provide for the indemnification of our directors and officers in a variety of circumstances, which may include in-demnification for liabilities under the Securities Act. . . . Weight Watchers also carries insurance on behalf of its directors, officers, employees or agents that may cover liabilities under the Securities Act. . . .

ITEM 15.   RECENT SALES OF UNREGISTERED SECURITIES.

During the three years preceding the filing of this registration statement, the Registrant sold shares of and issued options for its common stock and preferred stock in the amounts, at the times, and for the aggregate amounts of consideration listed below without registration under the Securities Act of 1933. Exemption from registration under the Securities Act for each of the following sales is claimed under Section 4(2) of the Securities Act because each of the transactions was by the issuer and did not involve a public offering: . . .

ITEM 16.   EXHIBITS AND FINANCIAL STATEMENT SCHEDULES.

(A) EXHIBITS

EXHIBIT NO.	DESCRIPTION OF EXHIBIT
1.1**	Form of Underwriting Agreement.
3.1**	Form of Amended and Restated Articles of Incorporation of Weight Watchers International, Inc.
3.2**	Form of Amended and Restated Bylaws of Weight Watchers International, Inc.
4.1	Senior Subordinated Dollar Notes Indenture. . . .
4.2	Guarantee Agreement. . . .
4.3	Senior Subordinated Euro Notes Indenture. . . .
4.4	Guarantee Agreement. . . .
4.5**	Form of Rights Agreement between Weight Watchers International, Inc. and EquiServe Trust Company, N.A.
4.6**	Specimen of stock certificate representing Weight Watchers International, Inc.'s common stock, no par value.
5.1**	Opinion of Hunton & Williams.
10.1**	Amended and Restated Credit Agreement. . . .
10.2	Preferred Stockholders' Agreement. . . .
10.3	Stockholders' Agreement. . . .
10.4	License Agreement, dated as of September 29, 1999, between WW Foods, LLC and Weight Watchers International, Inc. (Incorporated by reference to Exhibit 10.4 of Weight Watchers International, Inc.'s Form S-4 Registration Statement No. 333-92005).
10.5	License Agreement . . . between Weight Watchers International, Inc. and H.J. Heinz Company
10.6	License Agreement . . . between WW Foods, LLC and H.J. Heinz Company
10.7	LLC Agreement. . . .
10.8	Operating Agreement . . . between Weight Watchers International, Inc. and H.J. Heinz Company (Incorporated by reference to Exhibit 10.8 of Weight Watchers International, Inc.'s Form S-4 Registration Statement No. 333-92005).
10.9**	Stockholders' Agreement . . . among Weight Watchers International, Inc., Artal Luxembourg S.A., Merchant Capital, Inc., Logo Incorporated Pty. Ltd., Long Island International Limited, Envoy Partners and Scotiabanc, Inc. Registration Rights Agreement . . . among WeightWatchers.com, Inc., Weight Watchers International, Inc., H.J. Heinz Company and Artal Luxembourg S.A. . . . Stockholders' Agreement . . . among WeightWatchers.com, Weight Watchers International, Inc., Artal Luxembourg S.A. and H.J. Heinz Company. . . .
10.12	Letter Agreement. . . .

(B)   FINANCIAL STATEMENT SCHEDULE

Schedule II — Valuation and Qualifying Accounts — Period from December 30, 2000, and years ended December 30, 2000, April 23, 2000 and April 24, 1999 on page II-7.

REPORT OF INDEPENDENT ACCOUNTANTS
ON FINANCIAL STATEMENT SCHEDULE

To the Board of Directors of Weight Watchers International, Inc.:

Our audits of the consolidated financial statements referred to in our report dated March 2, 2001, except as to Note 21, which is as of November 14, 2001, appearing elsewhere in this Registration Statement also included an audit of the financial statement schedule listed in Item 16(b) of this Form S-1. In our opinion, this financial statement schedule presents fairly, in all material respects, the information set forth therein when read in conjunction with the related consolidated financial statements.

PricewaterhouseCoopers LLP
New York, New York
March 2, 2001

II-6

WEIGHT WATCHERS INTERNATIONAL, INC.
SCHEDULE II — VALUATION AND QUALIFYING ACCOUNTS

[Schedule Omitted—Eds.]

ITEM 17. UNDERTAKINGS.

Insofar as indemnification for liabilities arising under the Securities Act of 1933 (the "Securities Act") may be permitted to directors, officers and controlling persons of the registrant pursuant to the foregoing provisions, or otherwise, the registrant has been advised that in the opinion of the Securities and Exchange Commission such indemnification is against public policy as expressed in the Securities Act and is, therefore, unenforceable. In the event that a claim for indemnification against such liabilities (other than the payment by the registrant of expenses incurred or paid by a director, officer or controlling person of the registrant in the successful defense of any action, suit or proceeding) is asserted by such director, officer or controlling person in connection with the securities being registered, the registrant will, unless in the opinion of its counsel the matter has been settled by controlling precedent, submit to a court of appropriate jurisdiction the question whether such indemnification by it is against public policy as expressed in the Securities Act and will be governed by the final adjudication of such issue.

The undersigned registrant hereby undertakes that:

(1) For purposes of determining any liability under the Securities Act, the information omitted from the form of prospectus filed as part of this Registration Statement in reliance upon Rule 430A and contained in a form of prospectus filed by the registrant pursuant to Rule 424(b)(1) or

(4) or 497(h) under the Securities Act shall be deemed to be part of this Registration Statement as of the time it was declared effective.

(2) For the purpose of determining any liability under the Securities Act, each post-effective amendment that contains a form of prospectus shall be deemed to be a new registration statement relating to the securities offered therein, and the offering of such securities at that time shall be deemed to be the initial bona fide offering thereof.

SIGNATURES

Pursuant to the requirements of the Securities Act, the registrant has duly caused this Amendment No. 3 to the Registration Statement to be signed on its behalf by the undersigned, thereunto duly authorized on November 14, 2001.

WEIGHT WATCHERS INTERNATIONAL, INC.
By: *
_____

Linda Huett
President, Chief Executive Officer and
Director

Pursuant to the requirements of the Securities Act, as amended, this Amendment No. 3 to the Registration Statement has been signed below by the following persons in the capacities indicated on the 14th day of November, 2001.

SIGNATURE	TITLE
* _____ Linda Huett	President, Chief Executive Officer and Director
* _____ Thomas S. Kiritsis	Vice President and Chief Financial Officer
* _____ Raymond Debbane	Chairman of the Board of Directors
* _____ Sacha Lainovic	Director

```
——————————*—————————— Director
       Christopher J. Sobecki


——————————*—————————— Director
       Jonas M. Fajgenbaum
```

By: **/s/ SACHA LAINOVIC**
          ATTORNEY-IN-FACT

Rule 424(b)(1) Prospectus Filed by Weight Watchers International, Inc.

FILED PURSUANT TO RULE 424(b)(1)
REGISTRATION NO. 333-69362

17,400,000 Shares

[LOGO]
Common Stock

The shares of common stock are being sold by the selling share-holders named in this prospectus. We will not receive any of the proceeds from the shares of common stock sold by the selling shareholders.

Prior to this offering, there has been no public market for our common stock. Our common stock has been authorized for listing on the New York Stock Exchange under the symbol "WTW."

The underwriters have an option to purchase a maximum of 2,610,000 additional shares from certain of the selling shareholders to cover over-allotments of shares.

Investing in our common stock involves risks. See "Risk Factors" beginning on page 8.

	Price to Public	Underwriting Discounts and Commissions	Proceeds to Selling Shareholders
Per Share	$24.00	$1.26	$22.74
Total	$417,600,000	$21,924,000	$395,676,000

Delivery of the shares of common stock will be made on or about November 20, 2001.

UNDERWRITING

Under the terms and subject to the conditions contained in an underwriting agreement dated November 14, 2001, the selling shareholders have agreed to sell to the underwriters named below, for whom Credit Suisse First Boston Corporation and Goldman, Sachs & Co. are acting as representatives, the following respective numbers of shares of common stock:

UNDERWRITER	NUMBER OF SHARES
Credit Suisse First Boston Corporation	3,809,750
Goldman, Sachs & Co.	3,809,750
Merrill Lynch, Pierce, Fenner & Smith Incorporated	2,643,500
Salomon Smith Barney Inc.	2,643,500
UBS Warburg LLC	2,643,500
ABN AMRO Rothschild LLC	100,000
Banc of America Securities LLC	100,000
Bear, Stearns & Co. Inc.	100,000
Deutsche Banc Alex. Brown Inc.	100,000
A.G. Edwards & Sons, Inc.	100,000
Invemed Associates LLC	100,000
Lehman Brothers Inc.	100,000
J.P. Morgan Securities Inc.	100,000
Prudential Securities Incorporated	100,000
RBC Dain Rauscher Inc.	100,000
Scotia Capital (USA) Inc.	100,000
U.S. Bancorp Piper Jaffray Inc.	100,000
Robert W. Baird & Co. Incorporated	50,000
Davenport & Company LLC	50,000
Gruntal & Co., LLC	50,000
Janney Montgomery Scott LLC	50,000
Johnston, Lemon & Co. Incorporated	50,000
Edward D. Jones & Co., L.P.	50,000
C.L. King & Associates, Inc.	50,000
Legg Mason Wood Walker, Incorporated	50,000
Parker/Hunter Incorporated	50,000
Raymond James & Associates, Inc.	50,000
Sanders Morris Harris	50,000
SunTrust Capital Markets, Inc.	50,000
The Williams Capital Group, L.P.	50,000
Total	$17,400,000

Certain of the selling shareholders have granted to the underwriters a 30-day option to purchase on a pro rata basis up to an aggregate of 2,610,000 additional shares at the initial public offering price less the underwriting discounts and commissions. The option may be exercised only to cover any over-allotments of common stock.

The underwriters propose to offer the shares of common stock initially at the public offering price on the cover page of this prospectus and to selling group members at that price less a selling concession of $0.756 per share. The underwriters and selling group members may allow a discount of $0.10 per share on sales to other broker/dealers. After the initial public offering the representatives may change the public offering price and concession and discount to broker/dealers.

The following table summarizes the compensation the selling shareholders will pay and the estimated expenses we will pay:

| | | PER SHARE | TOTAL |
WITHOUT OVER-ALLOTMENT	WITH OVER-ALLOTMENT	WITHOUT OVER-ALLOTMENT	WITH OVER-ALLOTMENT
Underwriting discounts and commissions paid by selling shareholders			
$1.26	$1.26	$21,924,000	$25,212,600
Expenses payable by us			
$0.12	$0.11	$2,230.563	$2,250.563

The representatives have informed us that the underwriters do not expect discretionary sales to exceed 5% of the shares of common stock being offered.

F. Public Offers by Seasoned and Well-Known Seasoned Issuers

1. Integrated Disclosure for the Seasoned Company

Page 184.   Add the following after Note 3:

3. *Registration of Asset-Backed Securities.* Since 2004, Regulation AB provides a comprehensive regime for the registration, disclosure, reporting and communications with respect to public offerings of asset-backed securities. Responding to multiple issues that contributed to the collapse of market for asset-backed securities in 2008 and the ensuing financial crisis, the SEC in 2014 substantially revised Regulation AB. SEC Securities Act Rel. No. 9638 (August 2014). The new rules apply to public offerings of ABS backed by residential mortgages, commercial mortgages, auto loans and leases, and debt securities. The new rules do not apply to exempt offerings, such as those carried out pursuant to Rule 144A, discussed in Chapter 6. New Regulation AB requires issuers to provide an expanded amount of standardized asset-level data to be provided in both prospectuses and periodic reports. These disclosures occur pursuant to Forms SF-1 and SF-3 (something of the parallel to Forms S-1 and S-3). Most ABS public offerings are shelf offerings and prior to the 2014 revision they occurred on Form S-3 which was available provided the ABS was rated "investment grade." The new rule abandons ratings as the gateway for ABS shelf offerings, limits ABS shelf offerings to Form SF-3, and condition eligibility to use Form SF-3 on:

- Certification by the issuer's CEO that the CEO is familiar with certain factors about the offering and ABS such as the prospectus, assets involved, structure of offering, material transaction documents as well as stating the CEO has a reasonable basis to conclude the securitization is structure to produce cash flows in amounts sufficient to service scheduled payments
- The transaction provides the appointment of an "asset representations reviewer" who will conduct a review of compliance representations and any warranties made with respect to the pool of assets
- The transaction documents include a dispute resolution mechanism and provision of a mechanism to accommodate requests by investors to communicate with other investors

An important feature of new Regulation AB is the introduction of "speed bumps" in the offering process. For example, a preliminary prospectus must be filed with the SEC at least three business days prior to the first sale of any security in the offering; the SEC otherwise does not require such a filing prior to sales from the shelf. The intent of this change is to provide investors with additional time to assess the assets underlying the offering. And, any material change to the preliminary prospectus must be reflected in that prospectus 48 hours prior to the first sale.

Regulation AB now requires extensive data (asset-level "data points") regarding the underlying assets so that investors can assess the credit quality of the assets. These disclosures are to be made in machine-readable format (XML) so that the information can be downloaded for analysis. Among the required asset-level data points to be provide are: information bearing on the payment stream of underlying assets such as contractual terms, payment schedule, interest rate calculations, and whether payments are scheduled to change over time; collateral supporting asset; geography of debtor and collateral; valuation of collateral; loan-to-value ratios; loss mitigation arrangements; and the extent of verification of debtors' income and employment status. Aside from enhanced disclosure focused on the underlying assets, Regulation AB requires extensive disclosure of those involved in the offering and their various undertakings, such as any power to modify the composition of the underlying assets or agreement to repurchase underlying assets as well as how similar pool (called "static pools") of assets by the ABS' sponsors has performed.

G.   Shelf Registration Under Rule 415

Page 194.   Add the following new section at the end of the page:

5.   Who's Liable For Misrepresentations at the Takedown?

Federal Housing Finance Agency v. HSBC North America Holdings, Inc.
2013 U.S. Dist. LEXIS 175287 (Dec. 2013)

DENISE COTE, District Judge:

. . .

These actions involve alleged misrepresentations in the offering materials for residential mortgage backed securities purchased by Fannie Mae and Freddie Mac (collectively, the "GSEs") between 2005 and 2007. The securities at issue consisted of certificates issued by a trust that were backed by pools of underlying mortgages and entitled the owners to income in the form of payments on those mortgages. The value of the certificates thus depended on the ability of mortgagors to repay the loan principal and interest and the adequacy of the collateral in the event of default.

The certificates purchased by the GSEs were issued pursuant to shelf registration statements filed with the Securities and Exchange Commission ("SEC"), prospectuses, and prospectus supplements that together constitute the "offering documents" for each security. The alleged misrepresentations at the heart of these cases concerned the creditworthiness of the borrowers and the quality of the collateral underlying the certificates and were made in the prospectus supplements; the original registration statements contained only a base prospectus with generic information about future offerings. . . .

The instant motion for judgment on the pleadings . . . is brought by certain individual defendants who signed the relevant shelf registration statements but did not sign the prospectus supplements (the "Individual Defendants"). The Individual Defendants argue that they cannot be liable under *Section 11* for misstatements contained in the prospectus supplements.

DISCUSSION

. . .

The shelf registration process allows certain would-be issuers to file a generic registration statement with the SEC that omits the type of detailed information that must generally be disclosed to purchasers. . . . Once this "shelf registration statement" becomes effective, the issuer can take the registration statement "off the shelf," make the required supplemental disclosures, and use the shelf registration statement to issue securities whenever it chooses, without the need for further SEC action. Thus, as in this case, a single shelf registration statement may be used for a series of offerings. . . .

In 2005, the SEC promulgated *Rule 430B*, which among other things broadened the category of disclosures that can be made in prospectus supplements rather than post-effective amendments to registration statements. . . . In a motion to dismiss filed in 2012 in one of these coordinated actions, certain defendants argued that FHFA's claims were time-barred because the effective dates of the certificates at issue were the dates of the underlying registration statements, not the dates they were actually marketed to the public. See *FHFA v. UBS, 2012 U.S. Dist. LEXIS 88471, 2012 WL 2400263, at *1*. The Court rejected this argument, noting that *Rule 430B* did not change the rule that "[a] filing that represents a fundamental change in the information set forth in the registration statement has always been deemed to restart the clock on Section 11 claims." . . . Because the prospectus supplements at issue in these cases were plainly "fundamental changes" to the information contained in the registration statements, the Court held, they triggered new Securities Act liability periods. . . . The defendants did not then argue, and the Court therefore did not address, the issue of what effect *Rule 430B* has on Section 11 liability for individuals who sign registration statements but not later prospectus supplements that contain alleged misstatements.

Section 11 creates liability for signers of registration statements whenever "any part of the registration statement, when such part became effective, contained an untrue statement of material fact or [omission]." *15 U.S.C. § 77k(a)* (emphasis added). Under *Rule 430B*, information in a prospectus supplement required to be filed by *Rule 424(b)(2), (b)(5)*, or *(b)(7)* is "deemed to be part of and included in the registration statement on the earlier of the date such subsequent form of prospectus is first used or the date and time of the first contract of sale of securities in the offering to which such subsequent form of prospectus relates." *17 C.F.R. § 230.430B(f)(1).* These Rule 424(b) sections cover prospectus supplements that disclose information previously omitted from the prospectus filed as part of an effective registration statement pursuant to the shelf registration process. *17 C.F.R. § 230.424(b)(2).*

Because *Rule 430B* "deems newly disclosed information to be included in the registration statement, plaintiffs may base claims under *§ 11* of the '33 Act on a supplemental prospectus's material misstatements or omissions." . . . Indeed, in its release accompanying *Rule 430B*, the SEC explained that "[a]s a result of *Rule 430B* . . . prospectus supplements required to be filed under *Rule 424* . . . will, in all cases, be deemed to be part of and included in registration statements for purposes of Securities Act *Section 11*." Securities Offering Reform, SEC Release Nos. 33-8591 . . .

The instant motion, however, focuses on a wrinkle in this regime. *Rule 430B* drew a distinction between different categories of potential *Section 11* defendants in determining whether the filing of a prospectus supplement triggers a new "effective date." Under *Rule 430B(f)(2)*, the date the prospectus supplement is first used (or the date the securities to which it relates are first sold) becomes the new "effective date" of the registration statement for purposes of Section 11 liability "of the issuer and any underwriter at the time only." Id. at *§ 230.430B(f)(2)* (emphasis added). As to directors, "the date a form of prospectus is deemed part of and included in the registration statement . . . shall not be an effective date established pursuant to *paragraph (f)(2)* of the section." Id. at *§ 230.430B(f)(4)*.

Were that the end of the matter, *Rule 430B* would have effected a sea change in the Section 11 liability of directors, exempting them from responsibility for the material contained in later-filed prospectus supplements. But, it is not. *Rule 430B* included two exceptions in *paragraph (f)(4)*, which provide that the filing of a prospectus supplement creates a new effective date for directors when it is filed "for purposes of including information required by *section 10(a)(3)* of the Act or pursuant to Item *512(a)(1) (ii)* of Regulation S-K." *17 C.F.R. § 230.430B(f)(4)*. Item *512(a)(1)(ii)*, in turn, requires a registrant to "reflect in the prospectus any facts or events arising after the effective date of the registration statement . . . which, individually or in the aggregate, represent a fundamental change in the information set forth in the registration statement." *17 C.F.R. § 229.512(a)(1)(ii)*.

Where the prospectus supplement represents a "fundamental change" to the information in the registration statement, then, even for directors, it is "deemed part of and included in the registration statement on the earlier of the date such subsequent form of prospectus is first used or the date and time of the first contract of sale of securities in the offering to which such subsequent form of prospectus relates." *17 C.F.R. § 230.430B(f)(1)* and *(f)(4)*. Thus, a prospectus supplement containing information representing a fundamental change in the information provided in the registration statement creates Section 11 liability for directors based on that new information.

. . .

[T]he prospectus supplements here certainly constituted fundamental changes to the information previously disclosed about the certificates, as they contained virtually all of the detail about the underlying collateral and the ability of borrowers to repay the loans that would have been material to investors. . . . *Rule 430B* therefore does not exempt the Individual Defendants from Section 11 liability for misstatements contained in the prospectus supplements.

||5||

Exempt Transactions

B. The Intrastate Offering Exemption: Section 3(a)(11)

2. The Rule 147 Safe Harbor

Page 260.   Add the following update at the end of the excerpt from Release No. 34-5450:

Update: The SEC has proposed changes in Rule 147 that will convert the rule from a safe harbor for the Section 3(a)(11) exemption to an SEC administrative exemption promulgated under Section 28 of the '33 Act. See Release No. 33-9973 (Oct. 30, 2015). The proposal would offer a new federal exemption that dovetails with the increasing number of states adopting crowdfunding exemptions under state laws.

The proposed changes would keep an intra-state focus for Rule 147 without some of the limitations imposed by Section 3(a)(11) that have limited the usefulness of the exemption. For example, under the proposal general and solicitation and advertising activities are allowed and offers need not be strictly limited to residents of the state (the rule will require that all purchasers be residents). Along a similar line, the proposed rule redefines what is meant by an intrastate offering and eases the standards by which an issuer will be deemed to be doing business in the state. The proposed rule limits the availability of the exemption to offerings that are either registered in the state in which all of the purchasers are resident or conducted pursuant to an exemption from state law registration in such state that limits the amount of securities an issuer may sell to no more than $5 million in a twelve-month period and imposes an investment limitation on investors.

D. Regulation D and the Limited Offering Exemptions

1. An Overview of Regulation D

Page 279. Add the following update at the end of the summary overview of Regulation D:

Update: The SEC has proposed raising the cap on the maximum amount of securities that may be sold in any twelve month period under Rule 504 from the current $1 million limitation to $5 milllion. *See* Release No. 33-9973 (Oct. 30, 2015). The proposal, if adopted, also will disqualify certain "bad actors" from participating in Rule 504 offerings.

5. Limitations on the Manner and Scope of an Offering

e. The 2012 Reforms (The JOBS Act and Proposed Rule 506(c)

Page 293. Replace this section with the following:

e. The 2012 Reforms (The JOBS Act and Rule 506(c))

For years, commentators have criticized the SEC's broad ban on general solicitations.[1] A recent ABA committee report criticized the emphasis on pre-existing relationships as an independent factor in determining the availability of the exemption. See Committee on Federal Regulation of Securities, ABA Section of Business Law, 66 Bus. Law. 85 (2010). The report suggested that the limitations on general solicitation and general advertising do not reflect a current environment in which "it is hard to control faxes, e-mails, and text messaging and, even more, their forwarding."

---

1 *See, e.g.,* Cohn & Yadley, Capital Offense: The SEC's Continuing Failure to Address Small Business Financing Concerns, 4 N.Y.U. J. L. & Bus. 10, 11-12 (2007) (criticizing the general solicitation ban on numerous grounds, including its elimination of the Internet as an important source of financing); Orcutt, Improving the Efficiency of the Angel Finance Market: A Proposal to Expand the Intermediary Role of Finders in the Private Capital Raising Setting, 37 Ariz. St. L.J. 861, 943-944 (2005) (noting "angel" investors who invest at the earliest stages of start-ups often prefer to do so anonymously and that this, combined with the general solicitation ban, creates substantial impediments to issuers seeking investors); Langevoort, Angels on the Internet: The Elusive Promise of "Technological Disintermediation" for Unregistered Offerings of Securities, 2 J. Small & Emerging Bus. L. 1, 25-26 (1998) (any form of general solicitation should be allowed so long as the offering is made available only to accredited investors).

Although the SEC has resisted revisiting the broad ban on general solicitations, reformers were able to partially secure their objectives through Congressional action. The Jumpstart Our Business Startups (JOBS) Act directed the Commission to amend Regulation D to provide that Rule 502(c)'s ban on general solicitations or general advertising does not apply to offers and sales under Rule 506, provided that all purchasers are accredited investors. The legislation, which does not address the applicability of Rule 502(c) to the exemptions under Rules 504 and 505, also directs the SEC to require that issuers take reasonable steps to verify the status of purchasers as accredited investors.

The relaxation of general solicitation restrictions has generated considerable excitement in the investment community. Enthusiasm is dampened somewhat, however, by the legislation's requirement that issuers must take reasonable steps to verify that all purchasers are accredited. As was discussed above, Regulation D's accredited investor definition is satisfied if either the investor satisfies the standards of Rule 501(a) or the issuer reasonably believes that the investor satisfies these standards. The JOBS Act mandate adds the additional and potentially more onerous requirement that issuers actually take steps to verify that investors are accredited.

The SEC has issued final rules implementing the legislative direction on general solicitations in some Rule 506 offerings. See Release No. 33-9415 (July 10, 2013). Under a new Rule 506(c), an issuer may employ a general solicitation or advertising to offer and sell securities if three conditions are satisfied: (1) the issuer takes reasonable steps to verify that purchasers are accredited investors; (2) all purchasers are accredited investors, either because they qualify under the criteria of Rule 501(a) or because the issuer reasonably believes they qualify; and (3) other applicable conditions of Regulation D are satisfied. Alternatively, an issuer pursing a Rule 506 offering may opt to include investors who are not accredited investors and/ or not take steps to verify that all investors are accredited, but in such a case the offering must proceed under 506(b) where the restrictions on general solicitation and advertising continue to apply.

The steps that must be taken to verify status of purchasers as accredited investors has been the issue of greatest concern to the investment community. When it proposed Rule 506(c), the SEC opted for a flexible approach keying on "principles-based methods of verification." To this end, the release accompanying the proposal suggested three factors (the list is nonexclusive) that may be relevant in evaluating the reasonableness of steps taken:

> 1. *The nature of the purchaser and the type of accredited investor the purchaser claims to be.* Steps necessary to verify the status of a broker-dealer (e.g., simply going to FINRA's BrokerCheck website) differ from the steps necessary to verify the assets and liabilities of a natural person claiming to be an accredited investor.

2. The amount and type of information that the issuer has about the purchaser. An issuer may rely on publicly available information (e.g., public filings revealing an individual is an executive officer) and third party information providing "reasonably reliable" evidence that an individual falls within one of the categories of accredited investors (e.g., an industry publication that discloses annual compensation of an individual at a level exceeding the income threshold for an accredited investor).

3. The nature and terms of the offering. An issuer that solicits investors through a website accessible to the general public or through a widely disseminated email or social media solicitation presumably must take greater measures to verify accredited investors than an issuer that solicits investors from a database of pre-screened accredited investors. As to the terms of the offering, imposition of a high minimum investment standard that could only be met by an accredited investor could be a relevant factor in versification of accredited investor status.

The proposed rule's approach to verification of accredited investor status was controversial. The flexible facts and circumstances approach preserves the SEC's enforcement options but leaves issuers wondering what, exactly, is expected of them in order to satisfy the new verification requirements. In particular, many commenters urged the Commission to establish concrete safe harbors that would allow issuers to proceed with some assurance that they have taken the reasonable steps that are required in order to verify the accredited status of an investor.

In finalizing Rule 506(c), the SEC opted to retain the flexible principles-based methods of verifying accredited investor status. The final rule, however, adds four non-exclusive safe harbors designed to give issuers greater certainty that they have done what is necessary to verify the status of an investor. The safe harbors include:

1. For verifying whether an investor is accredited based on income, the issuer may review tax forms or filings that substantiate income, together with a written representation from the investor that he or she has a reasonable expectation of reaching the income level necessary to qualify as an accredited investor during the current year.
2. For verifying whether an investor is accredited based on net worth, the issuer may review documents substantiating assets (e.g., bank and brokerage statements, tax assessments, and third party appraisals). As to liabilities, a consumer report and written statement of the investor that all liabilities have been disclosed are required.
3. The issuer may obtain a written confirmation from a registered broker-dealer, an SEC-registered investment adviser, a licensed attorney, or a certified public accountant that such person or entity has taken reasonable steps to verify that the purchaser is an accredited

investor within the prior three months and has determined that the purchaser is an accredited investor.

4. For any natural person who invested in an issuer's Rule 506(b) offering as an accredited investor prior to the effective date of Rule 506(c) and remains an investor of the issuer, the issuer may rely on a certification by the investor that he or she qualifies as an accredited investor.

As to the first three methods of verifying that an investor is accredited, the Commission noted:

> [W]e believe that there will likely be few instances in which [any of these three methods] would not constitute reasonable steps to verify accredited investor status. With respect to the verification method for the income test, there are numerous penalties for falsely reporting information in an Internal Revenue Service form, and these forms are filed with the Internal Revenue Service for purposes independent of investing in a Rule 506(c) offering. Similarly, we believe that the various forms of documentation set forth in the verification method for the net worth test ordinarily are generated for reasons other than to invest in a Rule 506(c) offering (with the possible exception of appraisal reports) and, in combination with a consumer report and a written representation from the investor regarding his or her liabilities, constitute sufficiently reliable evidence that such person's net worth exceeds $1 million, excluding the value of the person's primary residence. With respect to the third-party verification method, we have included written confirmations from certain third parties in our non-exclusive list of verification methods because these third parties are subject to various regulatory and/or licensing requirements. . . .

Release No. 33-9415 (July 10, 2013).

Concern over the relaxed restrictions on general solicitations implemented through new Rule 506(c) prompted the NASAA to issue an investor advisory:

> Historically, private placement offerings have been sold through familiar sources such as the recommendation of a friend, a broker-dealer, or members of a church or other social organizations. These sales rely upon directed communication and trusted relationships. Now, private placement offerings may be sold through unknown sources by such means as cold calls or free lunch seminars that may use high pressure sales tactics and impose artificial time limits in an effort to hurry the investment decision.

North American Securities Administrators Association, Informed Investor Advisory: Private Placement Offerings (2013).

On the same day it finalized the general solicitation rule changes, the Commission proposed additional Regulation D amendments requiring issuers to file a Form D fifteen days before engaging in a general solicitation and an updated Form D within thirty days of the closing of the offering. The proposed rules further require that all solicitation and advertising materials be submitted to the SEC and include stringent one-year disqualification provisions applicable to issuers or their affiliates who fail to comply with the filing requirements. The proposed rules are controversial, and concern over their impact if adopted in the form proposed has dampened enthusiasm over the relaxation of solicitation and advertising restrictions for offerings under the new Rule 506(c).

8.   Additional Regulation D Requirements and Features

b.   *"Bad Actor" Disqualifiers*

Page 303.   Replace this section with the following:

Until recently, Rule 505 stood alone among the Regulation D exemptions in including "bad actor" disqualifiers also applicable to Regulation A offerings, discussed infra. Absent a waiver by the SEC, Rule 505 is unavailable for the securities of any issuer described in Rule 262 of Regulation A. Briefly, this limitation will arise if the issuer; a predecessor of the issuer; an affiliated issuer; an underwriter; a director, an officer, or a general partner of the issuer; or a 10 percent or greater shareholder has engaged in certain conduct that violates federal securities laws. Since the disqualification provisions of Rule 505(b)(2)(iii) operate without regard to the issuer's reasonable belief, considerable care must be exercised to investigate the backgrounds of relevant parties to ensure the exemption is not lost by virtue of the bad boy disqualifiers. Even established brokerage firms are not immune from bad boy disqualifying conditions, a fact that can be seen in the numerous requests (mostly successful) in recent years for SEC waivers. See, e.g., Goldman Sachs & Co., SEC No-Action Letter (April 12, 2012); J.P. Morgan Securities LLC, SEC No-Action Letter (July 8, 2011).

Section 926 of the Dodd-Frank Wall Street Reform and Consumer Protection Act of 2010 directed the Commission to develop bad actor disqualification rules applicable to Rule 506 offerings. In response, the SEC approved a new Rule 506(d) implementing disqualifiers but also including a reasonable care exception that will protect the issuer from losing the exemption if it shows that it did not know and, in the exercise of reasonable care, could not have known of the disqualifying event. See Securities Act Release No. 33-9414 (July 10, 2013).

On the advisability of extending bad actor disqualifiers to Rule 504 offerings, see Brown, Seed Capital, Rule 504 and the Applicability of Bad Actor Provisions (February 8, 2012) (online at SSRN: http://ssrn.com/abstract=2001529).

E.   *The Crowdfunding Exemption*

Page 313.   **Add the following update to the crowdfunding discussion.**

In a 686 page release, the Commission finalized the long-awaited crowdfunding rules. See SEC Release No. 33-9974 (Oct. 30, 2015). The following is a summary of the features of the new rules.

Offering Size.   A $1 million cap on the aggregate amount sold by the issuer in any twelve month period includes all amounts sold under the Section 4(a)(6) crowdfunding exemption but does not include amounts sold under another exemption. Moreover, a crowdfunded offering will not be integrated with another exempt offering made by the issuer. The Commission cautioned that "[a]n issuer conducting a concurrent exempt offering for which general solicitation is not permitted, however, would need to be satisfied that purchasers in that offering were not solicited by means of the offering made in reliance on Section 4(a)(6)." Similarly, any concurrent exempt offering for which general solicitation is permitted may not include an advertisement of the terms of an offering made in reliance on Section 4(a)(6) unless the advertisement complied with the crowdfunding rules.

Holding Period.   One year holding period (subject to limited exceptions).

Investment Limitations.   The rule addresses the statute's ambiguous investment limitations when an investor's annual income exceeds $100,000 but net worth does not, or vice versa. It employs a sliding scale metric keyed to net worth and income thresholds. Under this approach, if either annual income or net worth is less than $100,000, then a limit of the greater of (1) $2,000, or (2) 5 percent of annual income or net worth (whichever is less) applies. If both net worth and annual income exceed $100,000, the investment cap (not to exceed $100,000) is ten percent of the lesser of the net worth or annual income. The issuer may rely on the intermediary to assess whether purchasers are within these limits.

Note the investment limitations as to a particular investor are applied in the aggregate across all crowdfunding offerings in which the investor participates over a twelve month period.

Business Plan.   The issuer must have a business plan, which need not be a formal document: "We understand that issuers engaging in crowdfunding transactions may have businesses at various stages of development in differing industries, and therefore, we believe that a specific 'business plan' could encompass a wide range of project descriptions, articulated ideas, and business models."

Disclosures.   The rules generally outline the types of disclosures an issuer must make, including information about officers, directors, and significant shareholders (and related parties transactions), description of business and business plan, use of proceeds, target offering amount and deadline, offering price and capital structure, and material risk factors, among other items. The disclosures are filed with the Commission on Form C.

Financial Statements.   To implement   Section 4A(b)(1)(D)'s requirement of a description of the financial condition of the issuer, the proposed rules outlined a tiered framework based on aggregate amounts offered over a twelve month period:

1. For offerings of less than $100,000, the issuer must provide income and tax data from the issuer's tax return and financial statements certified by the chief executive officer.
2. For offerings between $100,000 and $500,000, the issuer must provide financial statements "reviewed" by a public accountant independent of the issuer.
3. For first-time offerings exceeding $500,000, the issuer must provide financial statements "reviewed" by a public accountant independent of the issuer. If the issuer has previously sold securities under the crowdfunding exemption, the financial statements must be *audited* by an independent accountant.

Ongoing Reporting Obligations.   An issuer that has completed a crowdfunded offering will be required to file a report on EDGAR annually. The required disclosures and financial statements would be similar to those required at the offering stage.

Intermediaries. An issuer must use a single intermediary. In the SEC's view, multiple intermediaries would make it more difficult for "members of the crowd to effectively share information, because essentially, there would be multiple 'crowds.'" Moreover, a single intermediary will facilitate use of the intermediary in securing the issuer's compliance with the rules.

The rules prohibit direct or indirect issuer advertising other than notices somewhat similar to "tombstone ads" identifying the intermediary and directing investors to that platform.

Any person acting as an intermediary must register with the SEC as a broker or as a funding portal, and in either case the intermediary must become a member of a registered national securities associations (currently, the only such association is FINRA). The intermediary must have a reasonable basis for believing the issuer is in compliance with crowdfunding rules.

Although the belief may be based on reasonable reliance on the issuer's representations unless the intermediary has reason to question the truthfulness or reliability of the representations, there are lingering concerns over uncertainties associated with possible due diligence obligations for intermediaries.

'34 Act Reporting Triggers.   To address the concern that a large number of small investors in a crowdfunding transactions may trigger '34 Act Section 12(g) reporting requirements (applicable when the issuer has a class of securities with more than 2,000 holders or more than 500 holders who are not accredited investors), the proposed rules exempt securities issued under the crowdfunding exemption from Section 12(g)'s record holder count.

On another front, several states have adopted crowdfunding exemptions for intrastate offerings. The Division of Corporation Finance has responded with an interpretation of the intrastate offering exemption safe harbor (Rule 147) indicating that use of a third party Internet portal to promote the offering is not necessarily incompatible with the federal intrastate offering exemption if adequate measures are taken to limit offers to persons resident of the state:

> In the context of an offering conducted in accordance with state crowdfunding requirements, such measures would include, at a minimum, disclaimers and restrictive legends making it clear that the offering is limited to residents of the relevant state under applicable law, and limiting access to information about specific investment opportunities to persons who confirm they are residents of the relevant state (for example, by providing a representation as to residence or in-state residence information, such as a zip code or residence address).

See SEC Division of Corporation Finance, Compliance and Disclosure Interpretations, Question 141.04 (April 21, 2014).

G.   *Regulation A: Mini-Registration*

Page 318.   **Delete the existing material in Section G and replace with the following:**

G.   *Regulation A: Mini-Registration*

Regulation A (Rules 251-263) is an administrative exemption promulgated under Section 3(b) of the Securities Act, which was substantially expanded by the JOBS Act through the addition of Section 3(b)(2) authorizing the SEC to exempt from registration a class of securities if the aggregate offering price of the issuance does not exceed $50 million. Regulation A results

in unrestricted securities and is available for primary or secondary offerings. The exemption is not available for offerings by reporting companies
under the '34 Act.

Prior to the JOBS Act and the SEC's finalization of new Regulation
A rules in 2015, the maximum offering under the exemption was $5 mil-
lion, which rendered the exemption relatively unattractive. See Campbell,
Regulation A: Small Businesses' Search for "A Moderate Capital," 31 Del.
J. Corp. L. 77 (2006). In the face of a continuing decline in the use of
Regulation A, due largely to the relative low offering ceiling, Congress
moved to revitalize the exemption by raising the offering threshold to
$50 million. The Commission's 2015 rulemaking dramatically restructures
Regulation A offerings into two tiers likely to prove far more popular than
the prior iteration of the exemption. *See* Securities Act Release No. 33-9741
(Mar. 25, 2015).

> *Tier 1 Offerings.*   Tier 1 is available for offerings up to $20 million
> (including no more than $6 million on behalf of sellers who are affiliates of
> the issuer) over a twelve month period. There are no qualification require-
> ments for investors or limits on the amount a person may invest. Compliance
> with state blue sky laws is required.
>
> *Tier 2 Offerings.*   Tier 2 (sometime informally referred to as Regulation
> A+) is available for offerings up to $50 million (including no more than
> $15 million on behalf of sellers who are affiliates of the issuer) over a twelve
> month period. There are no investment limitations for accredited investors.
> For an investor who is not accredited, the purchase limit is no more than: (a)
> 10% of the greater of the investor's annual income or net worth (for natural
> persons); or (b) 10% of the greater of the investor's annual revenue or net
> assets at fiscal year-end (for non-natural persons). The purchase limits do
> not apply to purchases of securities that will be listed on a national securities
> exchange. Tier 2 offerings are exempt from blue sky review.

Other features and requirements for Regulation A offerings (Tier 1
and Tier 2) include the following:

Resales.   In contrast with offerings under Regulation D, securities sold
under Regulation A are not restricted, which means they may be resold
immediately (resales by affiliates of the issuer may create complications,
discussed in Chapter 6).

Integration.   Rule 251(c) provides that Regulation A offerings will not
be integrated with either (1) any *prior* offerings or (2) *later* offerings that are
registered, made in reliance upon Rule 701 (compensatory benefit plans),
made in reliance upon Regulation S, made in reliance upon the crowdfunding exemption or, importantly, made more than six months after the
Regulation A offering. Rule 251(c) is particularly important in that it offers

"two-sided" integration protection, rather than the "one-sided" protection more generally offered in safe harbors (such as Regulation D).

To illustrate, assume two offerings, separated by seven months. The first is under the intrastate offering exemption of Section 3(a)(11), and the second is under Rule 505 of Regulation D. Regulation D's safe harbor (Rule 502(a)) operates to protect only the Rule 505 offering from the effects of earlier sales under the Section 3(a)(11) offering; it does nothing to protect the Section 3(a)(11) offering from the effects of later sales under the Rule 505 offering. Rule 251(c) of Regulation A, on the other hand, offers two-sided protection — that is, if the second offering is under Regulation A, not only will it be protected from integration with the earlier Section 3(a)(11) offering, but also the earlier offers and sales will be protected from integration with the later Regulation A offering. The availability of two-sided protection is one of the more attractive features of Regulation A. For an excellent discussion of this point, as well as other aspects of integration under Regulation A, see Bradford, Regulation A and the Integration Doctrine: The New Safe Harbor, 55 Ohio St. L.J. 255 (1994).

Filing and Disclosure Requirements. Rule 252 requires the filing of an Offering Statement (Form I-A) before a Regulation A offering may commence. Issuers that are first-time filers may file non-public drafts for review. The Offering Statement must be qualified by the SEC before any sales may be made.

It is the filing obligations with respect to the Offering Statement that give a Regulation A offering the character of a mini-registration. The content requirements of the Offering Statement are simpler than the counterpart requirements of a registration statement. For Tier 1 offerings, balance sheets and income statements for two years are required; audited financial statements are required only to the extent they exist having been prepared for other purposes. For Tier 2 offerings, audited balance sheets and income statements for two years are required. Moreover, Tier 2 offerings are subject to ongoing reporting requirements that include obligations to file annual and semi-annual reports (but not the quarterly reports required of reporting companies).

Testing the Waters. For many years, Rule 254 has allowed Regulation A issuers to "test the waters" by soliciting interest from prospective investors prior to filing Offering Statements. In the Commission's words:

> [O]ne of the major impediments to a Regulation A financing for a small startup or developing company with no established market for its securities, is the cost of preparing the mandatory offering statement. The full costs of compliance would be incurred without knowing whether there will be any investor interest in the company.

Securities Act Release No. 6949 (July 30, 1992). Regulation A's testing the waters provision addresses this problem by allowing issuer's to assess at an early stage investor interest in a proposed offering. This feature of Regulation A influenced 2012 legislative reforms streamlining public offerings for emerging growth companies (discussed in Chapter 4).

Regulation A allows issuers in either Tier 1 or Tier 2 offerings to solicit investor interest both before and after the Offering Statement is filed. The issuer must file with the SEC any existing testing the water materials together with the Offering Statement. Rule 255(b) specifies the content and required legends for the materials. If testing the water materials are used after the SEC filing, the issuer must include an Offering Circular (a somewhat abbreviated version of the Offering Statement) or information on where it may be obtained.

Altering Course After Testing the Waters. Suppose an issuer tests the waters and concludes before filing an Offering Statement that the Regulation A offering should not go forward. May the issuer then offer the securities under another exemption or as part of a registered offering? As to a registered offering, Rule 255(e) provides that, if the issuer in the abandoned Regulation A offering solicited interest only from qualified institutional buyers or institutional accredited investors, then the abandoned offering would not be integrated with the subsequent registered offering. If the issuer solicited more broadly, then integration will not occur if at least thirty days passes between the last solicitation of interest under Regulation A and the filing of the registration statement; if fewer than thirty days elapse, whether integration occurs will be evaluated under the general (and nebulous) integration factors applicable when a safe harbor is not available.

What if after testing the waters but before filing an Offering Statement the issuer decides to instead have a Regulation D offering? Because Rule 255(c) speaks to registered rather than exempt offerings, the issuer would look to the more general integration provisions of Rule 251(c) (discussed above). Although the Rule provides for non-integration of Regulation A offerings with certain other listed offerings, a subsequent Regulation D offering is not one of those specifically listed, which means the cautious issuer will probably choose to avoid integration problems by waiting six months before proceeding with the Regulation D offering.

Disqualification.   Rule 262 includes the so-called bad actor disqualifiers that deny the exemption when the issuer or those closely associated with it have engaged in certain types of misconduct.

Substantial Compliance.   Regulation A includes a substantial compliance provision similar to that of Regulation D. Under Rule 260, failure to comply with a requirement of Regulation A will not result in loss of the exemption as to a particular purchaser if the issuer acted in good faith, the deviation was insignificant in relation to the offering as a whole, and the requirement not observed was not intended to protect the purchaser complaining of the deviation.

NOTES

1. State Regulation.   One reason for the limited use of Regulation A prior to its revitalization under the JOBS Act was that securities offered under the exemption were not covered securities and, therefore, were subject to state regulation. The final rules partially address this perceived problem by exempting Tier 2 offerings from state regulation (treating *all* offerees and purchasers under the offerings as "qualified purchasers" of covered securities).

Not surprisingly, the North American Securities Administrators Association, the voice of state regulators, has opposed the preemption of state law for Tier 2 offerings. Hoping to forestall the preemption, NASAA announced prior to the finalization of the Regulation A rules that its members had approved a streamlined multi-state review protocol that will allow a Regulation A filing to be made in one place and distributed electronically to all states. A lead examiner will be appointed as the primary point of contact for a filer, and each state will be allowed only 10 business days for review. This move, however, did not dissuade the SEC from exempting in the final rules Tier 2 offerings from state blue sky regulation.

2. Is Regulation A Attractive?   Regulation A should become very competitive with other exemptions. For example, when compared with offerings under Rules 504 and 505, a Regulation A Tier 1 offering may follow testing the waters and is not subject to the general solicitation restrictions or Rule 505's numerical limits on non-accredited investors. Moreover Regulation A results in unrestricted securities that are freely tradable.

Similarly, Regulation A Tier 2 offerings offer some advantages over Rule 506 offerings. Rule 506(b) offerings are subject to the ban on general solicitations and advertising, and the more lenient Rule 506(c) limits offerings to accredited investors. An issuer in a Regulation A Tier 2 offering may test the waters before filing, and the status of an investor as accredited is irrelevant (although purchasers are subject to the investment limits). As is the case with Tier 1, Tier 2 offerings result in unrestricted securities.

But there are some drawbacks to Regulation A when compared to the Regulation D exemptions. For example, Regulation A, like Rule 504 but unlike Rules 505 and 506, is not available to reporting companies. Moreover, Regulation A requires an offering statement and a Form 1A filing, and audited financial statements are required for Tier 2 offerings (as well as Tier 1 offerings when the statements are otherwise available).

Although issuers in Rule 506 offerings customarily provide some disclosures even when not required, issuers in Regulation A Tier 2 offerings are subject to initial and ongoing reporting requirements.

Regulation A also offers an attractive alternative to an IPO. The costs for the Regulation A offering (including legal counsel and auditors) will be lower. Form IA is a simpler filing than a registration statement, and SEC review will be quicker.

PROBLEMS

5-41. Brocon is proceeding with a Tier 1 Regulation A offering of common stock that will include a large number of investors who are not accredited. One of the likely investors is Carl, whose annual income as a high school teacher is $60,000. Carl is a friend of one of Brocon's officers. Carl has no investing experience but is interested in purchasing $20,000 of stock in the offering. Is there anything about Carl that should concern Brocon? What if it is a Tier 2 offering?

5-42. On April 1, Limitbeat, Inc. begins testing the waters for a $15 million Regulation A offering. On May 1 (the date the last prospective purchaser was contacted), it decides to scrap the Regulation A offer and proceed with a registered public offering. What is the earliest point at which it may safely file a registration statement without concern that the earlier Regulation A solicitation activities would constitute "gun jumping?" What if Limitbeat decides instead to proceed with a Rule 506 offering? *See* Rules 251(c), 254(c).

5-43. On March 1, Hightech, Inc. completed a $5 million Rule 505 offering. On November 1, it commences a Regulation A Tier 1 offering. How large may the Regulation A offering be? *See* Rule 251(a).

H.   Section 3(b)(2): Regulation A Plus

Page 322.   Delete this section.

‖6‖

Secondary Distributions

C.   Control Person Distributions

Page 360.   Add the following to the end of Note 3:

In World Trade Financial Corp. v. SEC, 793 F.3d 1243 (9th Cir. 2014), the court affirmed the SEC's decision to uphold substantial sanctions FINRA imposed against a broker who violated Section 5 in selling 2.3 million shares on behalf of three related sellers. In concluding that the broker failed to make a reasonable inquiry in connection with the resales, the Ninth Circuit emphasized the broker ignored numerous red flags such as the issuer was a recently established development stage company, the issuer's stock had just began to trade publicly, the stock was thinly traded, and the issuer had recently undergone a stock split in connection with its reverse merger. The court reasoned:

> [W]here, as here, there are numerous red flags indicating suspicious circumstances, a more searching inquiry is required. *See Wonsover, 205 F.3d at 415* (requiring a "searching inquiry" where unfamiliar shareholders offered the broker "a substantial block of little-known and thinly traded security" under questionable circumstances). Petitioners did not inquire into the origins of the iStorage stock despite the significant red flags that we have identified. The circumstances called for a more diligent inquiry, and Petitioners did not satisfy their duty.

What result if the broker in World Trade Financial Corp. executed numerous trades on behalf of the three customers in reliance on letters prepared by their attorney that their resale did not violate Section 5? *Cf.* SEC v. CMKM Diamonds, Inc., (9th Cir. 2013) (reversing grant of summary judgment to the SEC on whether transfer agent was a "substantial factor" in another's violation of section 5 when the agent, relying on two attorney opinion letters, issued shares without restrictive legends that were exchanged for previously restricted shares and their holders subsequently sold them in the market in violation of Section 5).

Page 377.   Substitute the following headings after Problem 6-27:

E.   Resales to QIBs and Accredited Investors

1.   Facilitating an Institutional Market for Unregistered Securities with Rule 144A

Page 382.   Add the following to Note 5:

The SEC amended rule 144A(d)(1) to remove references to "offer" and "offeree" so that securities can be offered to investors who are not QIBs as long as the securities are sold only to persons the seller reasonably believes are QIBs. In adopting the change, the SEC stated that such general solicitation and general advertisements in connection with Rule 144A will not affect the availability of the Section 4(a)(2) exemption for the initial sale of securities by issuers to initial purchasers. *See* Securities Act Rel. No. 9415 (July 10, 2013).

Page 383.   Add the following subsection within E. Resales to QIBs and Accredited Investors after Problem 6-30:

2.   Resales to Accredited Investors

In 2015, Section 4(a)(7) was added to the Securities Act establishing a new resale transaction exemption. The exemption is available to any seller except the issuer or its subsidiary and is conditioned on each purchaser being accredited and there being no general solicitation or general advertisement in connection with the resale. Note that the prohibition against general solicitation and advertisement parallels the same prohibition in Rule 502(c) of Regulation D. The exemption provided in Section 4(a)(7) is purchaser, not offeree, based, so that a selling shareholder does not violate Section 5 if she mistakenly offers, but does not sell, shares, to a person who is not accredited so long as those to whom shares are sold are accredited. Section 4(a)(7) does impose a modest information requirement, but only if the issuer is not a reporting company. When the issuer is not a reporting company certain basic information about the issuer as well as financial statements prepared according to generally accepted accounting principles

(IFRs in the case of foreign issuers), must be made available to the purchaser. The prohibition of general advertisement and solicitations unquestionably embraces the extensive guidance the SEC has provided through its no-action letters in connection with the similar prohibition in Rule 502(c) of Regulation D where the SEC has consistently emphasized the importance of a pre-existing relationship between buyer and seller. *Supra*, Chapter 5 D. 5. Limitations on the Manner and Scope of an Offering.

The resale exemption provided by Section 4(a)(7) is not constrained by the particular exemption the issuer relied upon to issue the shares. Furthermore, the selling shareholder is not subject to any required holding period. The shares acquired pursuant to Section 4(a)(7) are deemed to have been acquired "in a transaction not involving any public offering;" hence, shares acquired pursuant to Section 4(a)(7) are restricted for the purpose of later resale pursuant to Rule 144. Section 4(a)(7) does not apply if the seller or its agent is a "bad actor" as defined in Rule 506(d)(1) and does not apply if the issuer is a shell, blank check and blind pool company.

PROBLEMS

6-30A. Barney acquired 1000 SolarTech, Inc. shares from the issuer pursuant to an offering carried out in compliance with Rule 147. SolarTech is a reporting company. Four months later, Barney sold the shares to a business acquaintance, Alice, who lives in another state? Barney made no investigation of Alice's financial position; had he inquired he would have learned that Alice's net worth exceeded $1 million. Has Barney violated Section 5?

6-30B. What result in the preceding problem if Barney learned of Alice's interest in SolarTech through a local broker with whom both Barney and Alice had long-standing accounts? The broker acted as an intermediary and received his usual commission in connection with his efforts.

6-30C. When Barney sold his shares to Alice in Problem 6-30A, he genuinely believed SolarTech had complied with Rule 147. In fact, SolarTech's offering did not satisfy any exemption so that its offering violated Section 5. Does Barney sale violate Section 5?

6-30D. Assume that Barney acquired 1000 shares from SolarTech pursuant to a Rule 506 offering. Barney was among the few accredited investors who purchased in that offering. Four months later, he sold his shares to Sally, an accredited investor. In their negotiations leading up to the sale, Sally emailed Barney asking for information about SolarTech. Barney replied he had "not received any information about SolarTech when he made his own purchase." He copied SolarTech's corporate secretary on his response to Sally, asking that "relevant information" be sent to Sally. The corporate secretary emailed Sally a pdf file containing SolarTech's most recent customer catalog. Sally was impressed by the array of products and immediately purchased Barney's shares. Has Barney violated Section 5? Has Solar Tech violated Section 5?

F.   The Section 4 (1 ½) Exemption

Page 389.   Add the following after Note 6:

7. Section 4(a)(7): Congress' Complementary Rendering of 4 (1 ½).   In 2015, Section 4(a)(7) was added to the securities act authorizing a resale transaction exemption by any seller (other than issuers or a subsidiary of the issuer) provided each purchaser is accredited and there has not been any form of general solicitation or general advertisement. When the issuer is not a reporting company, certain information, including financial statements prepared according to generally accepted accounting principles (IFRs in the case of foreign issuers), must be made available to the purchaser. The shares acquired pursuant to Section 4(a)(7) are deemed to have been acquired "in a transaction not involving any public offering" and hence restricted for the purpose of later resale pursuant to Rule 144. Consider the ways in which Section 4(a)(7) is narrower than 4 (1 ½). Recall that the 4 (1 ½) exemption applies to resales by a control person and, among other features, is focused on buyer's sophistication, not accreditation status. Also, SEC no-action letters surrounding the scope of 4 (1 ½) permit advertisements to be used to place controlling blocks of shares. Section 4(a)(7) does not apply if the seller or its agent is a "bad actor" as defined in Rule 506(d)(1).

‖8‖
Exempt Securities

A. An Overview of Section 3

Page 434. **Add the following update to the discussion of Government Securities:**

Several important developments affecting municipal securities markets have occurred recently. The most notable is the bankruptcy of Detroit, with municipal bonds representing a portion of the city's estimated $18 billion debt. On the regulatory front, the SEC has charged the city of Miami with securities fraud in connection with several municipal bond offerings and related disclosures to investors. The Miami charges stem from the city's transfers of funds among internal accounts in order to mask increasing deficits in the General Fund, which is closely watched by investors as a barometer of the city's financial health.

‖9‖
Liability Under the Securities Act

A. Section 11

2. The Defendants and Their Defenses

NOTES AND QUESTIONS

Page 509   Replace note 4 with the following new note:

4. Opinions as Facts: The Omnicare Case.   In considering whether a state-ment by the Board of Directors that $54 per share in a proposed merger was a "fair" and "high" price could be a material *fact*, the Supreme Court in *Virginia Bankshares, Inc. v. Sandberg,* 501 U.S. 1083 (1991), held such a state-ment of opinion could be a fact for purposes of a Section 14 claim when there was objective evidence before the speaker that was inconsistent with the opinion expressed. The Supreme Court revisited opinion statements in *Omnicare, Inc. v. Laborers Dist. Council Constr. Indus. Pension Fund,* 135 S. Ct. 1318 (2015), in the context of the absolute liability standard imposed on issuers by Section 11. Purchasers of Omnicare's registered securities sued the company following the stock's dramatic price decline in the wake of a government suit claiming that Omnicare obtained business by paying kick-backs to various healthcare providers in violation of the law. Omnicare's registration statement stated:

> "We believe our contract arrangements with other healthcare providers, our pharmaceutical suppliers and our pharmacy practices are in compliance with applicable federal and state laws."

> "We believe that our contracts with pharmaceutical manufacturers are legally and economically valid arrangements that bring value to the healthcare sys-tem and the patients that we serve."

Omnicare carefully notes that Section 11(a) reaches not just "an untrue statements of a material fact" but also applies when there is a failure "to state a material fact . . . necessary to make the statements therein not misleading. The latter is generally understood to reach so-called half-truths. Here, Omnicare did not make "an untrue statement of material fact" as the plaintiff did not allege Omnicare officers acted fraudulently or recklessly (although the plaintiff did allege Omnicare's directors and officers "possessed reasonable grounds" for believing the professed opinions were truthful and complete). Of greater significance, examined more fully in Chapter 12, is *Omnicare's* holding with respect to examining opinion statements under the half-truth doctrine:

> [A]n investor cannot state a claim by alleging only that an opinion was wrong; the complaint must as well call into question the issuer's basis for offering the opinion. And to do so, the investor cannot just say that the issuer failed to reveal its basis. Section 11's omissions clause, after all, is not a general disclosure requirement; it affords a cause of action only when an issuer's failure to include a material fact has rendered a published statement misleading. . . . To be specific: The investor must identify particular (and material) facts going to the basis for the issuer's opinion—facts about the inquiry the issuer did or did not conduct or the knowledge it did or did not have—whose omission makes the opinion statement at issue misleading to a reasonable person reading the statement fairly and in context.

In remanding the case, the Supreme Court observed that the district court should determine whether the plaintiffs adequately alleged that Omnicare omitted warnings it had received from counsel that a particular contract carried a heightened risk of violating the anti-kickback laws and, if they so alleged, whether that omitted fact would have been material to reasonable investors so as to render the claims of legal compliance materially misleading.

‖10‖

Financial Innovation: Trading Markets, Derivatives, and Securitization

B.   Derivatives and Synthetic Investments

Page 570.   **Add the following new section following the carryover paragraph at the top of the page:**

5.   The "Volker Rule"

The recent financial crisis was fueled significantly by commercial banks directing significant sums of cash into speculative trading in a variety of financial products for their own accounts. Indeed, many believe the seeds of the financial crisis were sown in 1999 with Graham-Leach-Bliley Act's repeal of the Glass-Steagall Act that was enacted in the Great Depression that mandated a separation among commercial banking, investment banking, and insurance. With the disappearance of Glass-Steagall, universal banking arose whereby multiple financial activities were conducted within a single financial institution. Post 1999, banks increased in size, and an even more rapid increase occurred with respect to their deep engagement in speculative trading for their own accounts. Thus, concerns arose that financial institutions that held deposits of their banking customers placed those deposits at risk. The Volker Rule, believed by many to be not only the most complex but also the most contentious of the many provisions of

Dodd-Frank, was enacted to address concerns flowing from banks engaged in proprietary trading.

The Volker Rule consists of two broad prohibitions, each of which applies only to "banking entities."

- A banking entity may not sponsor or acquire an interest in a "covered fund"
- A banking entity may not engage in "proprietary trading"

In broad overview, a banking entity is an insured depository institution and the definition extends to any company that controls an insured depository institution or itself is an affiliate of either an insured depository institution or its control person.

The meaning of "covered fund" begins with the Investment Company Act of 1940. A covered fund is an entity that would otherwise fall with that Act as an investment company but for the exemption provided by either Section $3(c)(1)$ (i.e., the number of investors in the fund do not exceed 100) or $3(c)(7)$ (all fund investors are "qualified purchasers") of that Act. Correlatively, a fund that registers as an investment company under the Investment Company Act is exempt from the Volker Rule. As defined, any transaction in which a banking entity is involved that is using a privately offered entity that itself is relying on an Investment Company Act will be a covered fund; this means the Volker Rule reaches funds commonly known as hedge funds and private equity funds. Also included are "foreign funds" a designation that refers to an entity organized outside the U.S. that offers interests in the U.S. in reliance on either Section $3(c)(1)$ or $(3(c)(7)$; the scope of foreign bank is broader in the case of a U.S. organized or located banking entity as there is no requirement that interests be offered to investors in the U.S. or of any reliance on either of the two Investment Company Act exemptions. A final component of a covered fund is a commodity pool which depends on the definitions of commodity pool and commodity pool operator rules of the Commodity Futures Trading Commission.

As seen, the first Volker Rule prohibition is that of "sponsoring" a covered fund. Sponsorship is broadly defined and includes controlling the covered fund (e.g., selecting or having influence over a majority of its directors, trustees or managers), being its general partner, manager, or trustee, or even sharing its name (or some variant) with the fund for marketing purposes. One is not a sponsor, however, by providing investment advisory services to the covered fund.

The Volker Rule also prohibits a banking entity having an "ownership interest" in a covered fund. Such an interest extends beyond a typical proprietary interest such as a partnership and includes "other similar interests" such as the right to participate in the selection of the fund manager, right to share in the fund's income (however, the "carried interest" that fund advisors receive as compensation for profitable performance does not itself constitute an ownership interest), or a residual interest in fund assets upon its liquidation, or obtain a return based on fund performance. There is, however, subject to numerous qualifications, a de minimis exception that allows a banking entity to have an ownership interest in a covered fund of not more than 3 percent of the total ownership interest in a single fund. An important exception to being a covered fund exists in the case of asset-backed securities; the Volker Rule allows banking entities to sponsor or acquire an ownership interest in a covered fund that holds asset-backed securities comprised of loans, leases, receivables and certain high quality, highly liquid short-term investments. This exception thus allows banking entities to securitize their commercial and residential loans through CLOs and CDOs, respectively. A word of caution with this exception, and more broadly to the broad overview of a regulation that extends hundreds of pages in length: the exception established for CLOs and CDOs is quite intricate and detailed reflecting that under Dodd-Frank and even its final regulations, the various administrative agencies enjoy a significant amount of discretion as to the meaning of their intricate exceptions.

As stated earlier, the Volker Rule prohibits banking entities from acting as a principal in any transaction to purchase or sell any security, derivative, future or option on any security, derivative of future for the purpose of short-term resale. There is a rebuttable presumption that any such item (i.e., security, derivative, or future) held for 60 days or less involves prohibited proprietary trading. But even this statement has substantial qualifications. Major exceptions to the bar of proprietary trading are market making, trading in U.S. government obligations, underwriting, hedging, and trading on behalf of customers. Among the conditions to qualify for the market making exception is that the entity must hold itself out as willing to buy and sell positions in the particularly covered security, derivative, or future, that positions taken are not to exceed the near-term demands of customers or counterparties, and the revenue the banking entity derives is primarily from commissions including gains from bid/ask spreads. Most importantly, reliance on this exemption calls for active compliance efforts on the part of the bank. Another important exemption is hedging transactions. To qualify for this exemption, the trade must hedge an existing position or positions including a portfolio. To be a hedge the trade must be reasonably correlated to the risk intended to be hedge and subject to regular compliance review to assure written policies with respect to hedging are satisfied. The Volker Rule imposes monthly reporting of certain metrics to regulators with respect to market making, hedging, underwriting and trading in U.S. government securities. As seen, Volker Rule imposes on banking entities substantial new obligations with respect to maintaining active compliance obligations, including independent testing of compliance.

‖11‖

Financial Reporting: Mechanisms, Duties, and Culture

E. *The Management Discussion and Analysis Section of SEC Filings: Is Past Prologue*

Page 611.   Add the following to Note 2:

A very visible circuit split now exists with respect to whether Item 303 provides a disclosure duty that if not met gives rise to suit under Rule 10b-5. *Stratte-Mcclure v. Morgan Stanley*, 776 F.3d 94 (2nd Cir. 2015), holds that failure to satisfy the duty to disclose imposed by Item 303 supports the claim of a material omission in a private suit under Rule 10b-5. The Second Circuit reasoned, in part, that the failure to comply with Item 303 leads the reasonable investor to conclude there does not exist a known trend or uncertainty that management reasonably expects will have a material impact. In contrast, the Ninth Circuit in *Cohen v. NVIDIA*, 768 F.3d 1046 (9th Cir. 2014), reaffirmed its earlier position in *Verifone*, discussed earlier in this note.

|12|

Inquiries into the Materiality of Information

C. The "Total Mix" of Information and Market Efficiency

Page 642. Add the following new subsection at the bottom of the page:

3. Opinion Statements and Half-Truths

▌**Omnicare, Inc. v. Laborers Dist. Council Constr. Indus. Pension Fund**
Supreme Court of the United States 2015

JUSTICE KAGAN delivered the opinion of the Court.

Before a company may sell securities in interstate commerce, it must file a registration statement with the Securities and Exchange Commission (SEC). If that document either "contain[s] an untrue statement of a material fact" or "omit[s] to state a material fact . . . necessary to make the statements therein not misleading," a purchaser of the stock may sue for damages. . . . This case requires us to decide how each of those phrases applies to statements of opinion.

I. . . .

Section 11 thus creates two ways to hold issuers liable for the contents of a registration statement—one focusing on what the statement says and the other on what it leaves out. Either way, the buyer need not prove (as he must to establish certain other securities offenses) that the defendant acted with any intent to deceive or defraud. *Herman & MacLean* v. *Huddleston*, 459 U.S. 375, 381-382 . . . (1983).

This case arises out of a registration statement that petitioner Omnicare filed in connection with a public offering of common stock. Omnicare is the nation's largest provider of pharmacy services for residents of nursing homes. Its registration statement contained . . . analysis of the effects of various federal and state laws on its business model, including its acceptance of rebates from pharmaceutical manufacturers. . . . Of significance here, two sentences in the registration statement expressed Omnicare's view of its compliance with legal requirements:

- "We believe our contract arrangements with other healthcare providers, our pharmaceutical suppliers and our pharmacy practices are in compliance with applicable federal and state laws." . . .
- "We believe that our contracts with pharmaceutical manufacturers are legally and economically valid arrangements that bring value to the healthcare system and the patients that we serve." . . .

Accompanying those legal opinions were some caveats. On the same page as the first statement above, Omnicare mentioned several state-initiated "enforcement actions against pharmaceutical manufacturers" for offering payments to pharmacies that dispensed their products; it then cautioned that the laws relating to that practice might "be interpreted in the future in a manner inconsistent with our interpretation and application." . . . And adjacent to the second statement, Omnicare noted that the Federal Government had expressed "significant concerns" about some manufacturers' rebates to pharmacies and warned that business might suffer "if these price concessions were no longer provided." . . .

Respondents here, pension funds that purchased Omnicare stock in the public offering (hereinafter Funds), brought suit alleging that the company's two opinion statements about legal compliance give rise to liability under §11. Citing lawsuits that the Federal Government later pressed against Omnicare, the Funds' complaint maintained that the company's receipt of payments from drug manufacturers violated anti-kickback laws. . . . Accordingly, the complaint asserted, Omnicare made "materially false" representations about legal compliance. . . . And so too, the complaint continued, the company "omitted to state [material] facts necessary" to make its representations not misleading. . . . The Funds claimed that none of Omnicare's officers and directors "possessed reasonable grounds" for thinking that the opinions offered were truthful and complete. . . . Indeed, the complaint noted that one of Omnicare's attorneys had warned that a particular contract "carrie[d] a heightened risk" of liability under anti-kickback laws. . . . At the same time, the Funds made clear that in light of §11's strict liability standard, they chose to "exclude and disclaim any allegation that could be construed as alleging fraud or intentional or reckless misconduct." . . . .

The District Court granted Omnicare's motion to dismiss. See Civ. No. 2006-26 (ED Ky., Feb. 13, 2012) . . . . In the court's view, "statements regarding a company's belief as to its legal compliance are considered 'soft' information" and are actionable only if those who made them "knew [they] were untrue at the time." App. to Pet. for Cert. 38a. The court concluded that the Funds' complaint failed to meet that standard because it nowhere claimed that "the company's officers knew they were violating the law." *Id.*, at 39a. The Court of Appeals for the Sixth Circuit reversed. See 719 F. 3d 498 (2013). It acknowledged that the two statements highlighted in the Funds' complaint expressed Omnicare's "opinion" of legal compliance, rather than "hard facts." *Id.*, at 504 (quoting *In re Sofamor Danek Group Inc.*, 123 F. 3d 394, 401-402 (CA6 1997)). But even so, the court held, the Funds had to allege only that the stated belief was "objectively false"; they did not need to contend that anyone at Omnicare "disbelieved [the opinion] at the time it was expressed." 719 F. 3d, at 506 (quoting *Fait* v. *Regions Financial Corp.*, 655 F. 3d 105, 110 (CA2 2011)).

We granted certiorari . . . to consider how §11 pertains to statements of opinion. We do so in two steps, corresponding to the two parts of §11 and the two theories in the Funds' complaint. We initially address the Funds' claim that Omnicare made "untrue statement[s] of . . . material fact" in offering its views on legal compliance. . . . We then take up the Funds' argument that Omnicare "omitted to state a material fact . . . necessary to make the statements [in its registration filing] not misleading." . . . Unlike both courts below, we see those allegations as presenting different issues. In resolving the first, we discuss when an opinion itself constitutes a factual misstatement. In analyzing the second, we address when an opinion may be rendered misleading by the omission of discrete factual representations. Because we find that the Court of Appeals applied the wrong standard, we vacate its decision.

II

The Sixth Circuit held, and the Funds now urge, that a statement of opinion that is ultimately found incorrect—even if believed at the time made—may count as an "untrue statement of a material fact." . . . As the Funds put the point, a statement of belief may make an implicit assertion about the belief's "subject matter": To say "we believe X is true" is often to indicate that "X is in fact true." . . . In just that way, the Funds conclude, an issuer's statement that "we believe we are following the law" conveys that "we in fact are following the law"—which is "materially false," no matter what the issuer thinks, if instead it is violating an anti-kickback statute. . . .

But that argument wrongly conflates facts and opinions. A fact is "a thing done or existing" or "[a]n actual happening." Webster's New International Dictionary 782 (1927). An opinion is "a belief[,] a view," or a "sentiment which the mind forms of persons or things." *Id.*, at 1509. Most important, a statement of fact ("the coffee is hot") expresses certainty about a thing, whereas a statement of opinion ("I think the coffee is hot") does not. See *ibid.* ("An opinion, in ordinary usage . . . does not imply . . . definiteness . . . or certainty"); 7 Oxford English Dictionary 151 (1933) (an opinion "rests[s] on grounds insufficient for complete demonstration"). Indeed, that difference between the two is so ingrained in our everyday ways of speaking and thinking as to make resort to old dictionaries seem a mite silly. And Congress effectively incorporated just that distinction in §11's first part by exposing issuers to liability not for "untrue statement[s]" full stop (which would have included ones of opinion), but only for "untrue statement[s] of . . . *fact.*" §77k(a) (emphasis added).

Consider that statutory phrase's application to two hypothetical statements, couched in ways the Funds claim are equivalent. A company's CEO states: "The TVs we manufacture have the highest resolution available on the market." Or, alternatively, the CEO transforms that factual statement into one of opinion: "I *believe*" (or "I think") "the TVs we manufacture have the highest resolution available on the market." The first version would be an untrue statement of fact if a competitor had introduced a higher resolution TV a month before—even assuming the CEO had not yet learned of the new product. The CEO's assertion, after all, is not mere puffery, but a determinate, verifiable statement about her company's TVs; and the CEO, however innocently, got the facts wrong. But in the same set of circumstances, the second version would remain true. Just as she said, the CEO really did believe, when she made the statement, that her company's TVs had the sharpest picture around. And although a plaintiff could later prove that opinion erroneous, the words "I believe" themselves admitted that possibility, thus precluding liability for an untrue statement of fact. That remains the case if the CEO's opinion, as here, concerned legal compliance. If, for example, she said, "I believe our marketing practices are lawful," and actually did think that, she could not be liable for a false statement of fact—even if she afterward discovered a longtime violation of law. Once again, the statement would have been true, because all she expressed was a view, not a certainty, about legal compliance.

That still leaves some room for §11's false-statement provision to apply to expressions of opinion. As even Omnicare acknowledges, every such statement explicitly affirms one fact: that the speaker actually holds the stated belief. . . . W. Keeton, D. Dobbs, R. Keeton, & D. Owen, Prosser and Keeton on the Law of Torts §109, p. 755 (5th ed. 1984) (Prosser and Keeton) ("[A]n expression of opinion is itself always a statement of . . . the fact of the belief, the existing state of mind, of the one who asserts it"). For that reason, the CEO's statement about product quality ("I believe our TVs have the highest resolution available on the market") would be an untrue statement of fact—namely, the fact of her own belief—if she knew that her company's TVs only placed second. And so too the statement about legal compliance ("I believe our marketing practices are lawful") would falsely describe her own state of mind if she thought her company was breaking the law. In such cases, §11's first part would subject the issuer to liability (assuming the misrepresentation were material).

In addition, some sentences that begin with opinion words like "I believe" contain embedded statements of fact—as, once again, Omnicare recognizes. . . . Suppose the CEO in our running hypothetical said: "I believe our TVs have the highest resolution available because we use a patented technology to which our competitors do not have access." That statement may be read to affirm not only the speaker's state of mind, as described above, but also an underlying fact: that the company uses a patented technology. . . . Accordingly, liability under §11's false-statement provision would follow (once again, assuming materiality) not only if the speaker did not hold the belief she professed but also if the supporting fact she supplied were untrue.

But the Funds cannot avail themselves of either of those ways of demonstrating liability. The two sentences to which the Funds object are pure statements of opinion: To simplify their content only a bit, Omnicare said in each that "we believe we are obeying the law." And the Funds do not contest that Omnicare's opinion was honestly held. Recall that their complaint explicitly "exclude[s] and disclaim[s]" any allegation sounding in fraud or deception. . . . What the Funds instead claim is that Omnicare's belief turned out to be wrong—that whatever the company thought, it was in fact violating anti-kickback laws. But that allegation alone will not give rise to liability under §11's first clause because, as we have shown, a sincere statement of pure opinion is not an "untrue statement of material fact," regardless whether an investor can ultimately prove the belief wrong. That clause, limited as it is to factual statements, does not allow investors to second-guess inherently subjective and uncertain assessments. In other

103

words, the provision is not, as the Court of Appeals and the Funds would have it, an invitation to Monday morning quarterback an issuer's opinions.

III

A

That conclusion, however, does not end this case because the Funds also rely on §11's omissions provision, alleging that Omnicare "omitted to state facts necessary" to make its opinion on legal compliance "not misleading."[3] As all parties accept, whether a statement is "misleading" depends on the perspective of a reasonable investor: The inquiry (like the one into materiality) is objective. . . . We therefore must consider when, if ever, the omission of a fact can make a statement of opinion like Omnicare's, even if literally accurate, misleading to an ordinary investor.

Omnicare claims that is just not possible. On its view, no reasonable person, in any context, can understand a pure statement of opinion to convey anything more than the speaker's own mindset. . . .

That claim has more than a kernel of truth. A reasonable person understands, and takes into account, the difference we have discussed above between a statement of fact and one of opinion. See *supra*, at 6-7. She recognizes the import of words like "I think" or "I believe," and grasps that they convey some lack of certainty as to the statement's content. See, *e.g.*, Restatement (Second) of Contracts §168, Comment *a*, p. 456 (1979) (noting that a statement of opinion "implies that [the speaker] . . . is not certain enough of what he says" to do without the qualifying language). And that may be especially so when the phrases appear in a registration statement, which the reasonable investor expects has been carefully word-smithed to comply with the law. When reading such a document, the investor thus distinguishes between the sentences "we believe X is true" and "X is true." And because she does so, the omission of a fact that merely rebuts the latter statement fails to render the former misleading. In other words, a statement of opinion is not misleading just because external facts show the opinion to be incorrect. Reasonable investors do not understand such statements as guarantees, and §11's omissions clause therefore does not treat them that way.

---

3. Section 11's omissions clause also applies when an issuer fails to make mandated disclosures—those "required to be stated"—in a registration statement. §77k(a). But the Funds do not object to Omnicare's filing on that score.

But Omnicare takes its point too far, because a reasonable investor may, depending on the circumstances, understand an opinion statement to convey facts about how the speaker has formed the opinion — or, otherwise put, about the speaker's basis for holding that view. And if the real facts are otherwise, but not provided, the opinion statement will mislead its audience. Consider an unadorned statement of opinion about legal compliance: "We believe our conduct is lawful." If the issuer makes that statement without having consulted a lawyer, it could be misleadingly incomplete. In the context of the securities market, an investor, though recognizing that legal opinions can prove wrong in the end, still likely expects such an assertion to rest on some meaningful legal inquiry — rather than, say, on mere intuition, however sincere.[5] Similarly, if the issuer made the statement in the face of its lawyers' contrary advice, or with knowledge that the Federal Government was taking the opposite view, the investor again has cause to complain: He expects not just that the issuer believes the opinion (however irrationally), but that it fairly aligns with the information in the issuer's possession at the time.[6] Thus, if a registration statement omits material facts about the issuer's inquiry into or knowledge concerning a statement of opinion, and if those facts conflict with what a reasonable investor would take from the statement itself, then §11's omissions clause creates liability.

An opinion statement, however, is not necessarily misleading when an issuer knows, but fails to disclose, some fact cutting the other way. Reasonable investors understand that opinions sometimes rest on a weighing of competing facts; indeed, the presence of such facts is one reason why an issuer may frame a statement as an opinion, thus conveying uncertainty. . . . Suppose, for example, that in stating an opinion about legal compliance, the issuer did not disclose that a single junior attorney expressed doubts about a practice's legality, when six of his more senior colleagues gave a stamp of approval. That omission would not make the statement of opinion misleading, even if the minority position ultimately proved correct:

---

5. In some circumstances, however, reliance on advice from regulators or consistent industry practice might accord with a reasonable investor's expectations.

6. The hypothetical used earlier could demonstrate the same points. Suppose the CEO, in claiming that her company's TV had the highest resolution available on the market, had failed to review any of her competitors' product specifications. Or suppose she had recently received information from industry analysts indicating that a new product had surpassed her company's on this metric. The CEO may still honestly believe in her TV's superiority. But under §11's omissions provision, that subjective belief, in the absence of the expected inquiry or in the face of known contradictory evidence, would not insulate her from liability.

A reasonable investor does not expect that *every* fact known to an issuer supports its opinion statement.[8]

Moreover, whether an omission makes an expression of opinion misleading always depends on context. Registration statements as a class are formal documents, filed with the SEC as a legal prerequisite for selling securities to the public. Investors do not, and are right not to, expect opinions contained in those statements to reflect baseless, off-the-cuff judgments, of the kind that an individual might communicate in daily life. At the same time, an investor reads each statement within such a document, whether of fact or of opinion, in light of all its surrounding text, including hedges, disclaimers, and apparently conflicting information. And the investor takes into account the customs and practices of the relevant industry. So an omission that renders misleading a statement of opinion when viewed in a vacuum may not do so once that statement is considered, as is appropriate, in a broader frame. The reasonable investor understands a statement of opinion in its full context, and §11 creates liability only for the omission of material facts that cannot be squared with such a fair reading.

These principles are not unique to §11: They inhere, too, in much common law respecting the tort of misrepresentation.[9] The Restatement of Torts, for example, recognizes that "[a] statement of opinion as to facts not disclosed and not otherwise known to the recipient may" in some circumstances reasonably "be interpreted by him as an implied statement" that the speaker "knows facts sufficient to justify him in forming" the opinion, or that he at least knows no facts "incompatible with [the] opinion." Restatement (Second) of Torts §539, p. 85 (1976).[10] When that is so, the

---

8. We note, too, that a reasonable investor generally considers the specificity of an opinion statement in making inferences about its basis. Compare two new statements from our ever-voluble CEO. In the first, she says: "I believe we have 1.3 million TVs in our warehouse." In the second, she says: "I believe we have enough supply on hand to meet demand." All else equal, a reasonable person would think that a more detailed investigation lay behind the former statement.

9. Section 11 is, of course, "not coextensive with common-law doctrines of fraud"; in particular, it establishes "a stringent standard of liability," not dependent on proof of intent to defraud. *Herman & MacLean* v. *Huddleston*, 459 U.S. 375, 381, 388-389 . . . (1983); see *supra*, at 2; *infra*, at 15, n. 11. But we may still look to the common law for its insights into how a reasonable person understands statements of opinion.

10. The Restatement of Contracts, discussing misrepresentations that can void an agreement, says much the same: "[T]he recipient of an assertion of a person's opinion as to facts not disclosed" may sometimes "properly interpret it as an assertion (a) that the facts known to that person are not incompatible with his opinion, or (b) that he knows facts sufficient to justify him in forming it." Restatement (Second) of Contracts §168, p. 455 (1979).

Restatement explains, liability may result from omission of facts — for example, the fact that the speaker failed to conduct any investigation — that rebut the recipient's predictable inference. See *id.*, Comment *a*, at 86; *id.*, Comment *b*, at 87. Similarly, the leading treatise in the area explains that "it has been recognized very often that the expression of an opinion may carry with it an implied assertion, not only that the speaker knows no facts which would preclude such an opinion, but that he does know facts which justify it." Prosser and Keeton §109, at 760. That is especially (and traditionally) the case, the treatise continues, where — as in a registration statement — a speaker "holds himself out or is understood as having special knowledge of the matter which is not available to the plaintiff." *Id.*, at 760-761 . . . .[11]

And the purpose of §11 supports this understanding of how the omissions clause maps onto opinion statements. Congress adopted §11 to ensure that issuers "tell[ ] the whole truth" to investors. H. R. Rep. No. 85, 73d Cong., 1st Sess., 2 (1933) (quoting President Roosevelt's message to Congress). For that reason, literal accuracy is not enough: An issuer must as well desist from misleading investors by saying one thing and holding back another. Omnicare would nullify that statutory requirement for all sentences starting with the phrases "we believe" or "we think." But those magic words can preface nearly any conclusion, and the resulting statements, as we have shown, remain perfectly capable of misleading investors. . . . Thus, Omnicare's view would punch a hole in the statute for half-truths in the form of opinion statements. And the difficulty of showing that such statements

---

11. In invoking these principles, we disagree with JUSTICE SCALIA's common-law-based opinion in two crucial ways. First, we view the common law's emphasis on special knowledge and expertise as supporting, rather than contradicting, [*30] our view of what issuers' opinion statements fairly imply. That is because an issuer has special knowledge of its business — including the legal issues the company faces — not available to an ordinary investor. Second, we think JUSTICE SCALIA's reliance on the common law's requirement of an intent to deceive is inconsistent with §11's standard of liability. As we understand him, JUSTICE SCALIA would limit liability for omissions under §11 to cases in which a speaker "subjectively intend[s] the deception" arising from the omission, on the ground that the common law did the same. *Post*, at 6 (opinion concurring in part and concurring in judgment) (emphasis deleted). But §11 discards the common law's intent requirement, making omissions unlawful — regardless of the issuer's state of mind — so long as they render statements misleading. See *Herman & MacLean*, 459 U.S., at 382, 103 S. Ct. 683, 74 L. Ed. 2d 548 (emphasizing that §11 imposes liability "even for innocent" misstatements or omissions). The common law can help illuminate when an omission has that effect, but cannot change §11's insistence on strict liability. See *supra*, at 14, n. 9.

are literally false—which requires proving an issuer did not believe them, . . . —would make that opening yet more consequential: Were Omnicare right, companies would have virtual *carte blanche* to assert opinions in registration statements free from worry about §11. That outcome would ill-fit Congress's decision to establish a strict liability offense promoting "full and fair disclosure" of material information. . . .

Omnicare argues, in response, that applying §11's omissions clause in the way we have described would have "adverse policy consequences." Reply Brief 17 . . . According to Omnicare, any inquiry into the issuer's basis for holding an opinion is "hopelessly amorphous," threatening "unpredictable" and possibly "massive" liability. . . .

Omnicare way overstates both the looseness of the inquiry Congress has mandated and the breadth of liability that approach threatens. As we have explained, an investor cannot state a claim by alleging only that an opinion was wrong; the complaint must as well call into question the issuer's basis for offering the opinion. . . . And to do so, the investor cannot just say that the issuer failed to reveal its basis. Section 11's omissions clause, after all, is not a general disclosure requirement; it affords a cause of action only when an issuer's failure to include a material fact has rendered a published statement misleading. . . . To be specific: The investor must identify particular (and material) facts going to the basis for the issuer's opinion—facts about the inquiry the issuer did or did not conduct or the knowledge it did or did not have—whose omission makes the opinion statement at issue misleading to a reasonable person reading the statement fairly and in context. . . . That is no small task for an investor.

. . .

Finally, we see no reason to think that liability for misleading opinions will chill disclosures useful to investors. Nothing indicates that §11's application to misleading factual assertions in registration statements has caused such a problem. And likewise, common-law doctrines of opinion liability have not, so far as anyone knows, deterred merchants in ordinary commercial transactions from asserting helpful opinions about their products. That absence of fallout is unsurprising. Sellers (whether of stock or other items) have strong economic incentives to . . . well, *sell* (*i.e.*, hawk or peddle). Those market-based forces push back against any inclination to underdisclose. And to avoid exposure for omissions under §11, an issuer need only divulge an opinion's basis, or else make clear the real tentativeness of its belief. Such ways of conveying opinions so that they do not mislead will keep valuable information flowing. And that is the only kind of information investors need. To the extent our decision today chills *misleading* opinions, that is all to the good: In enacting §11, Congress worked to ensure better, not just more, information.

B

Our analysis on this score counsels in favor of sending the case back to the lower courts for decision. . . . In doing so, however, we reemphasize a few crucial points pertinent to the inquiry on remand. Initially, as we have said, the Funds cannot proceed without identifying one or more facts left out of Omnicare's registration statement. . . . The Funds' recitation of the statutory language — that Omnicare "omitted to state facts necessary to make the statements made not misleading" — is not sufficient; neither is the Funds' conclusory allegation that Omnicare lacked "reasonable grounds for the belief" it stated respecting legal compliance. . . . At oral argument, however, the Funds highlighted another, more specific allegation in their complaint: that an attorney had warned Omnicare that a particular contract "carrie[d] a heightened risk" of legal exposure under anti-kickback laws. . . . On remand, the court must review the Funds' complaint to determine whether it adequately alleged that Omnicare had omitted that (purported) fact, or any other like it, from the registration statement. And if so, the court must determine whether the omitted fact would have been material to a reasonable investor — *i.e.*, whether "there is a substantial likelihood that a reasonable [investor] would consider it important." *TSC Industries*, 426 U.S., at 449 . . . .

Assuming the Funds clear those hurdles, the court must ask whether the alleged omission rendered Omnicare's legal compliance opinions misleading in the way described earlier — *i.e.*, because the excluded fact shows that Omnicare lacked the basis for making those statements that a reasonable investor would expect. . . . Insofar as the omitted fact at issue is the attorney's warning, that inquiry entails consideration of such matters as the attorney's status and expertise and other legal information available to Omnicare at the time. . . . Further, the analysis of whether Omnicare's opinion is misleading must address the statement's context. . . . That means the court must take account of whatever facts Omnicare *did* provide about legal compliance, as well as any other hedges, disclaimers, or qualifications it included in its registration statement. The court should consider, for example, the information Omnicare offered that States had initiated enforcement actions against drug manufacturers for giving rebates to pharmacies, that the Federal Government had expressed concerns about the practice, and that the relevant laws "could "be interpreted in the future in a manner" that would harm Omnicare's business. . . .

With these instructions and for the reasons stated, we vacate the judgment below and remand the case for further proceedings.

It is so ordered.

JUSTICE SCALIA, concurring in part and concurring in the judgment.

. . .

The Court's expansive application of §11's omissions clause to expressions of opinion produces a far broader field of misrepresentation; in fact, it produces almost the opposite of the common-law rule. The Court holds that a reasonable investor is right to expect a reasonable basis for *all* opinions in registration statements—for example, the conduct of a "meaningful . . . inquiry,"—unless that is sufficiently disclaimed. . . . Take the Court's hypothetical opinion regarding legal compliance. When a disclosure statement says "we believe our conduct is lawful," . . . the Court thinks this should be understood to suggest that a lawyer was consulted, since a reasonable investigation on this point would require consulting a lawyer. But this approach is incompatible with the common law, which had no "legal opinions are different" exception. See Restatement of Torts §545, at 102.

It is also incompatible with common sense. It seems to me strange to suggest that a statement of opinion as generic as "we believe our conduct is lawful" conveys the implied assertion of fact "we have conducted a meaningful legal investigation before espousing this opinion." It is strange to ignore the reality that a director might rely on industry practice, prior experience, or advice from regulators—rather than a meaningful legal investigation—in concluding the firm's conduct is lawful. The effect of the Court's rule is to adopt a presumption of expertise on all topics volunteered within a registration statement.

It is reasonable enough to adopt such a presumption for those matters that are required to be set forth in a registration statement. Those are matters on which the management of a corporation *are* experts. If, for example, the registration statement said "we believe that the corporation has $5,000,000 cash on hand," or "we believe the corporation has 7,500 shares of common stock outstanding," the public is entitled to assume that the management has done the necessary research, so that the asserted "belief" is undoubtedly correct. But of course a registration statement would never preface such items, within the expertise of the management, with a "we believe that." Full compliance with the law, however, is another matter. It is not specifically required to be set forth in the statement, and when management prefaces *that* volunteered information with a "we believe that," it flags the fact that this is not within our area of expertise, but we think we are in compliance.

Moreover, even if one assumes that a corporation issuing a registration statement is (by operation of law) an "expert" with regard to all matters stated or opined about, I would still not agree with the Court's disposition. The Court says the following:

"Section 11's omissions clause, as applied to statements of both opinion and fact, necessarily brings the reasonable person into the analysis, and asks what she would naturally understand a statement to convey beyond its literal meaning. And for expressions of opinion, that means considering the foundation *she would expect an issuer to have* before making the statement." . . . *Ante . . .* (emphasis added).

The first sentence is true enough—but "what she [the reasonable (female) person, and even he, the reasonable (male) person] would naturally understand a statement [of opinion] to convey" is not that the statement has the foundation *she* (the reasonable female person) considers adequate. *She* is not an expert, and is relying on the advice of an expert—who ought to know how much "foundation" is needed. She would naturally understand that the expert has conducted an investigation that *he* (or she or it) considered adequate. That is what relying upon the opinion of an expert means.

The common law understood this distinction. An action for fraudulent misrepresentation based on an opinion of an expert * was only allowed *when the expression of the opinion conveyed a fact*—the "fact" that summarized the expert's knowledge. Prosser and Keeton §109, at 761. And a fact was actionable only if the speaker *knew* it was false, if he *knew* he did not know it, or if he *knew* the listener would understand the statement to have a basis *that the speaker knew was not true.* Restatement of Torts §526, at 63-64. Ah!, the majority might say, so a speaker is liable for knowing he lacks *the listener's reasonable basis!* If the speaker *knows*—is actually aware—that the listener will understand an expression of opinion to have a specific basis that it does not have, then *of course* he satisfies this element of the tort.

But more often, when any basis is implied at all, both sides will understand that the speaker implied a "reasonable basis," but honestly disagree on what that means. And the common law supplied a solution for this: A speaker was liable for ambiguous statements—misunderstandings—as fraudulent misrepresentations *only* where he both knew of the ambiguity *and* intended that the listener fall prey to it. *Id.* §527, at 66. In other words, even assuming both parties *knew* (a prerequisite to liability) that the expression of opinion implied a "reasonable investigation," if the speaker and listener honestly disagreed on the nature of that investigation, the speaker was not liable for a fraudulent misrepresentation unless *he subjectively intended* the deception. And so in no circumstance would the listener's belief of a "reasonable basis" control: If the speaker subjectively believes he lacks a reasonable basis, then his statement is simply a knowing misrepresentation. *Id.* §526(a), at 63. If he does not know of the ambiguity, or knows of it, but does not intend to deceive, he is not liable. *Id.* §527, at 66. That his basis for belief was "objectively unreasonable" does not impart liability, so long as the belief was genuine.

This aligns with common sense. When a client receives advice from his lawyer, it is surely implicit in that advice that the lawyer has conducted a reasonable investigation—reasonable, that is, *in the lawyer's estimation.* The client is relying on the expert lawyer's judgment for the amount of investigation necessary, no less than for the legal conclusion. To be sure, if the lawyer conducts an investigation that he does not believe is adequate, he would be liable for misrepresentation. And if he conducts an investigation that he believes is adequate but is *objectively unreasonable* (and reaches an incorrect result), he may be liable for malpractice. But on the latter premise he is not liable for misrepresentation; all that was implicit in his advice was that he had conducted an investigation *he* deemed adequate. To rely on an expert's opinion is to rely on the expert's evaluation of *how much time to spend* on the question at hand.

The objective test proposed by the Court—inconsistent with the common law and common intuitions about statements of opinion—invites roundabout attacks upon expressions of opinion. Litigants seeking recompense for a corporation's expression of belief that turned out, after the fact, to be incorrect can always charge that even though the belief rested upon an investigation the corporation thought to be adequate, the investigation was not "objectively adequate."

. . . When an expert expresses an opinion instead of stating a fact, it implies (1) that he genuinely believes the opinion, (2) that he believes his basis for the opinion is sufficient, and (most important) (3) that he is not certain of his result. Nothing more. This approach would have given lower courts and investors far more guidance and would largely have avoided the Funds' attack upon Omnicare's opinions as though Omnicare held those opinions out to be facts.

I therefore concur only in part and in the judgment.

JUSTICE THOMAS, concurring in the judgment. (opinion omitted)

* * * *

Consider the future impact of *Omnicare* in light of the following:

Omnicare is important for opening up lines of attack against statements of opinion many lower courts had explicitly or implicitly, even if wrongly, given the strict liability standard, foreclosed by insisting on proof of subjective awareness of falsity [in reliance on the reasoning in *Virginia Bankshares* regarding the approach to opinion statements]. Some courts had extended this already powerful doctrine to expressions of "judgment" even when not explicitly prefaced by wors like "we believe." Most notable was the Second Circuit's decision in *Fait v. Regions Bank*, which held in the context of Section 11 that accountants' goodwill and loan loss reserve judgments were opinions. *Fait* became defense lawyers' "go to" citation for seeking dismissal of Section 11 claims of all sorts that might have some judgmental element to the alleged falsity. There is no better example of turning the text of Section

11 on its head, potentially constricting accountants' liability risk in ways that powerfully undermined the diligence-forcing role commonly ascribed to that provision. . . .

Omnicare did not directly address what constitutes an opinion, though the Court's discusson stressed the importance of words like "we believe" in signaling to readers some degree of uncertainty. . . . More clearly, *Omnicare* rejects the idea that the absence of dishonesty is a complete defense to opinion-based fraud; *Fait* assumed otherwise. At the very least, plaintiffs are now free to argue that the accountants' attestation or agreement as to the application of generally accepted accounting principles implied the absence of any facts that would seriously undermine the reasonableness of their exercise of discretion, whether or not those facts were actually known by the accountants. . . .

Sale & Langevoort, "We Believe": *Omnicare*, Legal Risk Disclosure and Corporate Governance, — Duke L. Journal — (forthcoming 2017).

D.   *Forward-Looking Information*

2.   **Statutory Safe Harbor for Forward-Looking Statements**

Page 658.   Add the following to Note 2:

See also, Arkansas Pub. Employees Ret. System v. Harman Int'l Indus., Inc., 791 F.3d 90 (D.C. Cir. 2015)(holding that cautionary language that misleads as to *facts* known to exist cannot provide a defense that the forward statement was accompanied by *meaningful* cautionary language).

E.   *The SEC and Corporate Governance*

2.   **The Interface of Materiality and Corporate Governance**

Page 681.   Add the following to the end of Note 2:

What if the disclosures that are compelled cast the registrant as being of a particularly ideological bent? The SEC's conflict mineral rules, described above, were upheld, except for the requirement that a registrant that could not, after a penetrating inquiry, conclude that its products were free of minerals from the Democratic Republic of Congo was required in its SEC filings to state that it could not state that its products were free of conflict minerals. The D.C. Circuit held this violated the registrant's First Amendment rights:

> That a disclosure is factual, standing alone, does not immunize it from scrutiny because "[t]he right against compelled speech is not, and cannot be, restricted to ideological messages." *Nat'l Ass'n of Mfrs.*, 717 F.3d at 957. . . . As the Supreme Court put it in *Riley v. National Federation of the Blind of North Carolina, Inc.*, the cases dealing with ideological messages "cannot be distinguished simply because they involved compelled statements of opinion while here we deal with compelled statements of 'fact.'" *487 U.S. 781, 797, 108 S. Ct. 2667, 101 L. Ed. 2d 669 (1988)*.
>
> . . . [I]t is far from clear that the description at issue – whether a product is "conflict free" – is factual and non-ideological. Products and minerals do not fight conflicts. The label "conflict free" is a metaphor that conveys moral responsibility for the Congo war. It requires an issuer to tell consumers that its products are ethically tainted, even if they only indirectly finance armed groups. An issuer, including an issuer who condemns the atrocities of the Congo war in the strongest terms, may disagree with that assessment of its moral responsibility. . . . By compelling an issuer to confess blood on its hands, the statute interferes with that exercise of the freedom of speech under the *First Amendment. See id.* . . .
>
> Under Central *Hudson*, the government must show (1) a substantial government interest that is; (2) directly and materially advanced by the restriction; and (3) that the restriction is narrowly tailored. *447 U.S. at 564-66; see R.J. Reynolds, 696 F.3d at 1212*. The narrow tailoring requirement invalidates regulations for which "narrower restrictions on expression would serve [the government's] interest as well." *Cent. Hudson, 447 U.S. at 565*. Although the government need not choose the "least restrictive means" of achieving its goals, there must be a "reasonable" "fit" between means and ends. *Bd. of Trs. v. Fox, 492 U.S. 469, 480, 109 S. Ct. 3028, 106 L. Ed. 2d 388 (1989)*. The government cannot satisfy that standard if it presents no evidence that less restrictive means would fail. *Sable Commc'ns v. FCC, 492 U.S. 115, 128-32, 109 S. Ct. 2829, 106 L. Ed. 2d 93 (1989)*.
>
> The Commission has provided no such evidence here. The Association suggests that rather than the "conflict free" description the statute and rule require, issuers could use their own language to describe their products, or the government could compile its own list of products that it believes are affiliated with the Congo war, based on information the issuers submit to the Commission. The Commission and Amnesty International simply assert that those proposals would be less effective. But if issuers can determine the conflict status of their products from due diligence, then surely the Commission can use the same information to make the same determination. And a centralized list compiled by the Commission in one place may even be more convenient or trustworthy to investors and consumers. The Commission has failed to explain why (much less provide evidence that)

the Association's intuitive alternatives to regulating speech would be any less effective.

Nat'l Assoc. of Mfgs. v. SEC, 748 F.3d 359 (D.C. Cir. 2014). Subsequently a redrafted rule was also struck down on First Amendment grounds. The court concluded the redrafted rule did not adequately identify an underlying governmental interest so that the rule could not be understood to alleviate the harm asserted to be remediated. Nat'l Ass'n of Mfgs. v. SEC, 800 F.3d 518 (D. C. Cir. 2015).

Page 684.   Add the following to Note 8:

In response to a Dodd-Frank mandate, the SEC added 402(u) to Regulation S-K requiring disclosure of median annual total compensation of all employees (excluding the CEO), the annual total compensation of the CEO, and the ratio of these two amounts. SEC, Pay Ratio Disclosure, Securities Act Rel. No 9877 (Aug. 5, 2015). The new disclosures become effective for existing companies in the first fiscal year on or after January 1, 2017. Emerging Growth Companies, smaller reporting companies, registered investment companies, and foreign private companies are exempt from the requirement.

The manner for determining the many factors that go into defining who is an employee and what is the "median employee's" compensation not surprisingly is technical. Essentially employees included in the calculation are all employees of the reporting company or any of its subsidiaries that, under accounting rules, are consolidated with the parent for financial reporting. The calculation includes employees who are full-time and part-time, seasonal and non-seasonal, as well as those inside and outside the U.S.(there is a de minimis exemption for foreign employees who collectively account for 5 percent or less of all employees). Total compensation may be annualized in the case of permanent employees who are not employed for the entire fiscal year. There is even the possibility of cost-of-living adjustments for employees that live in a jurisdiction other than where the CEO lives.

The regulations allow the "median employee" to be determined every three years, unless there has been a significant change in the company's employee population. While companies have flexibility in the way they can determine the median employee, such as by using statistical sampling, companies must disclose the methodology used to identify their median employee. Once the median employee is identified, the registrant must then calculate the median employee's compensation and briefly disclose the methodology by which total compensation was estimated.

3.   The Materiality of Being a "Bad" Citizen: Violations of State or Federal Law

Page 692.   Add the following to the end of Note 4:

Following a series of oil spills and significant governmental enforcement actions for multiple violations of environmental laws, a securities class action was filed against British Petroleum (BP). Among the statements targeted in the suit was the representation in BP's 2005 Annual Report: "Management believes that the Group's activities are in compliance in all material respects with applicable environmental laws and regulations." In finding the statement false, the Ninth Circuit reasoned as follows:

> Statements of legal compliance are pled with adequate falsity when documents detail specific violations of law that existed at the time the warranties were made. . . . Here, the complaint cites evidence of numerous violations, confirmed and alleged, of environmental laws and regulations, including: (1) the Clean Water Act, evidenced by BP's 2007 Guilty Plea with the DOJ; (2) Alaskan laws, evidenced by the company's civil settlement with the State; and (3) Pipeline Safety Laws, arising from BP-Alaska's failure to comply with . . . [various Corrective Action Orders issued by regulators]. Based on these allegations – the validity of which were ultimately confirmed by the company's guilty plea, consent decree, and millions of dollars in fines and penalties-defendants cannot say that they were in compliance, in all material respects, with applicable environmental laws and regulations. . . .
>
> Had BP actually complied with the Corrective Action Order at the time the statements were made, there may have been some basis for believing that BP had achieved "compliance in all material respects." But in this case, defendants had yet to take critical steps towards corrective action. . . .
>
> The next question is whether BP escapes possible liability by prefacing the statement with the phrase "management believes," and using the qualifier *material* compliance. . . .
>
> A statement of belief is a " 'factual' misstatement actionable under Section 10(b) if (1) the statement is not actually believed, (2) there is no reasonable basis for the belief, or (3) the speaker is aware of undisclosed facts tending seriously to undermine the statement's accuracy." *Kaplan v. Rose*, 49 F.3d 1363, 1375 (9th Cir. 1994) . . . The mere fact of ongoing "discussions" with regulators is insufficient to create a belief in "material compliance" with the law. Here, the violations of environmental law were egregious – BP had just spilled over 200,000 gallons of oil onto the Alaskan tundra in violation of the Clean Water Act. Its corrosion monitoring and leak detection systems fell

below industry standards and state requirements. And the discussions with regulators took place in the context of recent violations of the terms of the Corrective Action Order, imposed to mitigate "hazard[s] to life, property and the environment." Based on the pled facts, it is unclear how BP's management could consider the company to be "in compliance" or, alternatively, could view the violations to be immaterial.

For the foregoing reasons, we find that plaintiffs have adequately pled falsity.

Reese v. Malone, 2014 U.S. App. LEXIS 2747 (9th Cir. Feb. 13, 2014).

||13||

Fraud in Connection with the Purchase or Sale of a Security

F. Reliance

2. Open Market Frauds: The Fraud on the Market Theory

Page 740. Substitute the following for Basic Inc. v. Levinson:

|| **Halliburton Co. v. Erica P. John Fund, Inc.**
Supreme Court of the United States,
134 S. Ct. 2398

CHIEF JUSTICE ROBERTS delivered the opinion of the Court.

Investors can recover damages in a private securities fraud action only if they prove that they relied on the defendant's misrepresentation in deciding to buy or sell a company's stock. In *Basic Inc. v. Levinson, 485 U. S. 224 (1988)*, we held that investors could satisfy this reliance requirement by invoking a presumption that the price of stock traded in an efficient market reflects all public, material information—including material misstatements. In such a case, we concluded, anyone who buys or sells the stock at the market price may be considered to have relied on those misstatements.

We also held, however, that a defendant could rebut this presumption in a number of ways, including by showing that the alleged misrepresentation did not actually affect the stock's price — that is, that the misrepresentation had no "price impact." The questions presented are whether we should overrule or modify *Basic*'s presumption of reliance and, if not, whether defendants should nonetheless be afforded an opportunity in securities class action cases to rebut the presumption at the class certification stage, by showing a lack of price impact.

I

Respondent Erica P. John Fund, Inc. (EPJ Fund), is the lead plaintiff in a putative class action against Halliburton and one of its executives (collectively Halliburton) alleging violations of *section 10(b)* of the Securities Exchange Act of 1934 . . . and Securities and Exchange Commission *Rule 10b-5* . . . . According to EPJ Fund, between June 3, 1999, and December 7, 2001, Halliburton made a series of misrepresentations regarding its potential liability in asbestos litigation, its expected revenue from certain construction contracts, and the anticipated benefits of its merger with another company — all in an attempt to inflate the price of its stock. Halliburton subsequently made a number of corrective disclosures, which, EPJ Fund contends, caused the company's stock price to drop and investors to lose money.

EPJ Fund moved to certify a class comprising all investors who purchased Halliburton common stock during the class period. The District Court found that the proposed class satisfied all the threshold requirements of *Federal Rule of Civil Procedure 23(a)*: It was sufficiently numerous, there were common questions of law or fact, the representative parties' claims were typical of the class claims, and the representatives could fairly and adequately protect the interests of the class. . . . And except for one difficulty, the court would have also concluded that the class satisfied the requirement of *Rule 23(b)(3)* that "the questions of law or fact common to class members predominate over any questions affecting only individual members." . . . The difficulty was that Circuit precedent required securities fraud plaintiffs to prove "loss causation" — a causal connection between the defendants' alleged misrepresentations and the plaintiffs' economic losses — in order to invoke *Basic*'s presumption of reliance and obtain class certification. . . . Because EPJ Fund had not demonstrated such a connection for any of Halliburton's alleged misrepresentations, the District Court refused to certify the proposed class. . . . The United States Court of Appeals for the Fifth Circuit affirmed the denial of class certification on the same ground. . . . *597 F. 3d 330 (2010)*.

We granted certiorari and vacated the judgment, finding nothing in "*Basic* or its logic" to justify the Fifth Circuit's requirement that securities fraud plaintiffs prove loss causation at the class certification stage in order to invoke *Basic*'s presumption of reliance. *Erica P. John Fund, Inc.* v. *Halliburton*

Co., 563 U. S. ___, ___ (2011) (*Halliburton I*) (slip op., at 6). "Loss causation," we explained, "addresses a matter different from whether an investor
relied on a misrepresentation, presumptively or otherwise, when buying or
selling a stock." *Ibid.* We remanded the case. . . .

On remand, Halliburton argued that class certification was inappropriate because the evidence it had earlier introduced to disprove loss causation also showed that none of its alleged misrepresentations had actually
affected its stock price. By demonstrating the absence of any "price impact,"
Halliburton contended, it had rebutted *Basic*'s presumption that the members of the proposed class had relied on its alleged misrepresentations
simply by buying or selling its stock at the market price. And without the
benefit of the *Basic* presumption, investors would have to prove reliance on
an individual basis, meaning that individual issues would predominate over
common ones. The District Court declined to consider Halliburton's argument, holding that the *Basic* presumption applied and certifying the class
under *Rule 23(b)(3)*. . . .

The Fifth Circuit affirmed. *718 F. 3d 423 (2013)*. The court found that
Halliburton had preserved its price impact argument, but to no avail. *Id.,
at 435-436.* While acknowledging that "Halliburton's price impact evidence
could be used at the trial on the merits to refute the presumption of reliance," *id., at 433*, the court held that Halliburton could not use such evidence
for that purpose at the class certification stage, *id., at 435.* "[P]rice impact
evidence," the court explained, "does not bear on the question of common
question predominance [under *Rule 23(b)(3)*], and is thus appropriately considered only on the merits after the class has been certified." *Ibid.*

We once again granted certiorari, 571 U. S. ___ (2013), this time to
resolve a conflict among the Circuits over whether securities fraud defendants may attempt to rebut the *Basic* presumption at the class certification
stage with evidence of a lack of price impact. We also accepted Halliburton's
invitation to reconsider the presumption of reliance for securities fraud
claims that we adopted in *Basic*.

II

Halliburton urges us to overrule *Basic*'s presumption of reliance and
to instead require every securities fraud plaintiff to prove that he actually
relied on the defendant's misrepresentation in deciding to buy or sell a
company's stock. . . .

A

Section 10(b) of the Securities Exchange Act of 1934 and the Securities
and Exchange Commission's *Rule 10b-5* prohibit making any material

misstatement or omission in connection with the purchase or sale of any security. . . . To recover damages for violations of *section 10(b)* and *Rule 10b-5*, a plaintiff must prove " '(1) a material misrepresentation or omission by the defendant; (2) scienter; (3) a connection between the misrepresentation or omission and the purchase or sale of a security; (4) reliance upon the misrepresentation or omission; (5) economic loss; and (6) loss causation.' " *Amgen Inc.* v. *Connecticut Retirement Plans and Trust Funds*, 568 U. S. __, ___(2013). . . .

The reliance element " 'ensures that there is a proper connection between a defendant's misrepresentation and a plaintiff's injury.' " 568 U. S., at __ (slip op., at 4) (quoting *Halliburton I*, 563 U. S., at __ (slip op., at 4)). "The traditional (and most direct) way a plaintiff can demonstrate reliance is by showing that he was aware of a company's statement and engaged in a relevant transaction—*e.g.*, purchasing common stock—based on that specific misrepresentation." *Id.*, at ___ (slip op., at 4).

In *Basic*, however, we recognized that requiring such direct proof of reliance "would place an unnecessarily unrealistic evidentiary burden on the *Rule 10b-5* plaintiff who has traded on an impersonal market." *485 U. S., at 245.* That is because, even assuming an investor could prove that he was aware of the misrepresentation, he would still have to "show a speculative state of facts, *i.e.*, how he would have acted . . . if the misrepresentation had not been made." *Ibid.*

We also noted that "[r]equiring proof of individualized reliance" from every securities fraud plaintiff "effectively would . . . prevent[ ][plaintiffs] from proceeding with a class action" in *Rule 10b-5* suits. *Id., at 242.* If every plaintiff had to prove direct reliance on the defendant's misrepresentation, "individual issues then would . . . overwhelm[ ] the common ones," making certification under *Rule 23(b)(3)* inappropriate. *Ibid.*

To address these concerns, *Basic* held that securities fraud plaintiffs can in certain circumstances satisfy the reliance element of a *Rule 10b-5* action by invoking a rebuttable presumption of reliance, rather than proving direct reliance on a misrepresentation. The Court based that presumption on what is known as the "fraud-on-the-market" theory, which holds that "the market price of shares traded on well-developed markets reflects all publicly available information, and, hence, any material misrepresentations." *Id., at 246.* The Court also noted that, rather than scrutinize every piece of public information about a company for himself, the typical "investor who buys or sells stock at the price set by the market does so in reliance on the integrity of that price" — the belief that it reflects all public, material information. *Id., at 247.* As a result, whenever the investor buys or sells stock at the market price, his "reliance on any public material misrepresentations . . . may be presumed for purposes of a *Rule 10b-5* action." *Ibid.*

Based on this theory, a plaintiff must make the following showings to demonstrate that the presumption of reliance applies in a given case: (1) that the alleged misrepresentations were publicly known, (2) that they were material, (3) that the stock traded in an efficient market, and (4) that the plaintiff traded the stock between the time the misrepresentations were made and when the truth was revealed. See *id., at 248, n. 27; Halliburton I, supra*, at __ (slip op., at 5-6).

At the same time, *Basic* emphasized that the presumption of reliance was rebuttable rather than conclusive. Specifically, "[a]ny showing that severs the link between the alleged misrepresentation and either the price received (or paid) by the plaintiff, or his decision to trade at a fair market price, will be sufficient to rebut the presumption of reliance." *485 U. S., at 248.* So for example, if a defendant could show that the alleged misrepresentation did not, for whatever reason, actually affect the market price, or that a plaintiff would have bought or sold the stock even had he been aware that the stock's price was tainted by fraud, then the presumption of reliance would not apply. *Id., at 248-249.* In either of those cases, a plaintiff would have to prove that he directly relied on the defendant's misrepresentation in buying or selling the stock.

B

. . .

1

Halliburton first argues that the *Basic* presumption is inconsistent with Congress's intent in passing the 1934 Exchange Act. Because "[t]he *Section 10(b)* action is a 'judicial construct that Congress did not enact,'" this Court, Halliburton insists, "must identify—and borrow from—the express provision that is 'most analogous to the private 10b-5 right of action.'" Brief for Petitioners 12. . . . According to Halliburton, the closest analogue to *section 10(b)* is *section 18(a)* of the Act, which creates an express private cause of action allowing investors to recover damages based on misrepresentations made in certain regulatory filings. *15 U. S. C. §78r(a).* That provision requires an investor to prove that he bought or sold stock "in reliance upon" the defendant's misrepresentation. *Ibid.* In ignoring this direct reliance requirement, the argument goes, the *Basic* Court relieved *Rule 10b-5* plaintiffs of a burden that Congress would have imposed had it created the cause of action.

EPJ Fund contests both premises of Halliburton's argument, arguing that Congress has affirmed *Basic*'s construction of *section 10(b)* and that, in any event, the closest analogue to *section 10(b)* is not *section 18(a)* but *section 9, 15 U. S. C. §78i*—a provision that does not require actual reliance.

We need not settle this dispute. In *Basic,* the dissenting Justices made the same argument based on section 18(a) that Halliburton presses here. See *485 U. S., at 257-258* (White, J., concurring in part and dissenting in part). The *Basic* majority did not find that argument persuasive then, and Halliburton has given us no new reason to endorse it now.

2

Halliburton's primary argument for overruling *Basic* is that the decision rested on two premises that can no longer withstand scrutiny. The first premise concerns what is known as the "efficient capital markets hypothesis." *Basic* stated that "the market price of shares traded on well- developed markets reflects all publicly available information, and, hence, any material misrepresentations." *Id., at 246.* From that statement, Halliburton concludes that the *Basic* Court espoused "a robust view of market efficiency" that is no longer tenable, for " 'overwhelming empirical evidence' now 'suggests that capital markets are not fundamentally efficient.' " Brief for Petitioners 14-16 (quoting Lev & de Villiers, Stock Price Crashes and 10b-5 Damages: A Legal, Economic, and Policy Analysis, *47 Stan. L. Rev 7, 20 (1994)*). To support this contention, Halliburton cites studies purporting to show that "public information is often not incorporated immediately (much less rationally) into market prices." Brief for Petitioners 17; see *id., at 16-20.* See also Brief for Law Professors as *Amici Curiae* 15-18.

Halliburton does not, of course, maintain that capital markets are *always* inefficient. Rather, in its view, *Basic*'s fundamental error was to ignore the fact that " 'efficiency is not a binary, yes or no question.' " Brief for Petitioners 20 (quoting Langevoort, *Basic* at Twenty: Rethinking Fraud on the Market, *2009 Wis. L. Rev. 151, 167)*). The markets for some securities are more efficient than the markets for others, and even a single market can process different kinds of information more or less efficiently, depending on how widely the information is disseminated and how easily it is understood. . . . Yet *Basic,* Halliburton asserts, glossed over these nuances, assuming a false dichotomy that renders the presumption of reliance both underinclusive and overinclusive: A misrepresentation can distort a stock's market price even in a generally inefficient market, and a misrepresentation can leave a stock's market price unaffected even in a generally efficient one. Brief for Petitioners at 21.

Halliburton's criticisms fail to take *Basic* on its own terms. Halliburton focuses on the debate among economists about the degree to which the market price of a company's stock reflects public information about the company—and thus the degree to which an investor can earn an abnormal, above-market return by trading on such information. See Brief for Financial Economists as *Amici Curiae* 4-10 (describing the debate). That debate is not new. Indeed, the *Basic* Court acknowledged it and declined to enter the fray, declaring that "[w]e need not determine by adjudication what economists and social scientists have debated through the use of sophisticated statistical analysis and the application of economic theory." *485 U. S., at 246-247, n. 24.* To recognize the presumption of reliance, the Court explained, was not "conclusively to adopt any particular theory of how quickly and completely publicly available information is reflected in market price." *Id., at 248, n. 28.* The Court instead based the presumption on the fairly modest premise that "market professionals generally consider most publicly announced material statements about companies, thereby affecting stock market prices." *Id., at 247, n. 24. Basic*'s presumption of reliance thus does not rest on a "binary" view of market efficiency. Indeed, in making the presumption rebuttable, *Basic* recognized that market efficiency is a matter of degree and accordingly made it a matter of proof.

The academic debates discussed by Halliburton have not refuted the modest premise underlying the presumption of reliance. Even the foremost critics of the efficient-capital-markets hypothesis acknowledge that public information generally affects stock prices. See, *e.g.*, Shiller, We'll Share the Honors, and Agree to Disagree, N. Y. Times, Oct. 27, 2013, p. BU6 ("Of course, prices reflect available information"). Halliburton also conceded as much in its reply brief and at oral argument. See Reply Brief 13 ("market prices generally respond to new, material information"); Tr. of Oral Arg. 7. Debates about the precise *degree* to which stock prices accurately reflect public information are thus largely beside the point. "That the . . . price [of a stock] may be inaccurate does not detract from the fact that false statements affect it, and cause loss," which is "all that *Basic* requires." *Schleicher v. Wendt, 618 F. 3d 679, 685 (CA7 2010)*(Easterbrook, C. J.). Even though the efficient capital markets hypothesis may have "garnered substantial criticism since *Basic*," *post* . . . (THOMAS, J., concurring in judgment), Halliburton has not identified the kind of fundamental shift in economic theory that could justify overruling a precedent on the ground that it misunderstood, or has since been overtaken by, economic realities. . . .

Halliburton also contests a second premise underlying the *Basic* presumption: the notion that investors "invest 'in reliance on the integrity of [the market] price.' " . . . Halliburton identifies a number of classes of investors for whom "price integrity" is supposedly "marginal or irrelevant." . . . The primary example is the value investor, who believes that certain stocks are undervalued or overvalued and attempts to "beat the market" by buying the undervalued stocks and selling the overvalued ones. . . . See also Brief for Vivendi S. A. as *Amicus Curiae* 3-10 (describing the investment strategies of day traders, volatility arbitragers, and value investors). If many investors "are indifferent to prices," Halliburton contends, then courts should not presume that investors rely on the integrity of those prices and any misrepresentations incorporated into them. . . .

But *Basic* never denied the existence of such investors. As we recently explained, *Basic* concluded only that "it is reasonable to presume that *most* investors—knowing that they have little hope of outperforming the market in the long run based solely on their analysis of publicly available information—will rely on the security's market price as an unbiased assessment of the security's value in light of all public information." *Amgen*, 568 U. S., at ___ (slip op., at 5) (emphasis added).

In any event, there is no reason to suppose that even Halliburton's main counterexample—the value investor—is as indifferent to the integrity of market prices as Halliburton suggests. Such an investor implicitly relies on the fact that a stock's market price will eventually reflect material information—how else could the market correction on which his profit depends occur? To be sure, the value investor "does not believe that the market price accurately reflects public information *at the time he transacts.*" *Post*, at 11. But to indirectly rely on a misstatement in the sense relevant for the *Basic* presumption, he need only trade stock based on the belief that the market price will incorporate public information within a reasonable period. The value investor also presumably tries to estimate *how* undervalued or overvalued a particular stock is, and such estimates can be skewed by a market price tainted by fraud.

C . . .

Halliburton . . . argues that the *Basic* presumption cannot be reconciled with our recent decisions governing class action certification under *Federal Rule of Civil Procedure 23*. Those decisions have made clear that plaintiffs wishing to proceed through a class action must actually *prove*—not simply plead—that their proposed class satisfies each requirement of *Rule 23*, including (if applicable) the predominance requirement of *Rule 23(b)(3)*. See *Wal-Mart Stores, Inc.* v. *Dukes*, 564 U. S. ___, ___ (2011) (slip op., at 10); *Comcast Corp.* v. *Behrend*, 569 U. S. ___, ___ (2013) (slip op., at 5-6). According to Halliburton, *Basic* relieves *Rule 10b-5* plaintiffs of that burden, allowing courts to presume that common issues of reliance predominate over individual ones.

That is not the effect of the *Basic* presumption. In securities class action cases, the crucial requirement for class certification will usually be the predominance requirement of *Rule 23(b)(3)*. The *Basic* presumption does not relieve plaintiffs of the burden of proving—before class certification—that this requirement is met. *Basic* instead establishes that a plaintiff satisfies that burden by proving the prerequisites for invoking the presumption—namely, publicity, materiality, market efficiency, and market timing. The burden of proving those prerequisites still rests with plaintiffs and (with the exception of materiality) must be satisfied before class certification. *Basic* does not, in other words, allow plaintiffs simply to plead that common questions of reliance predominate over individual ones, but rather sets forth what they must prove to demonstrate such predominance.

Basic does afford defendants an opportunity to rebut the presumption of reliance with respect to an individual plaintiff by showing that he did not rely on the integrity of the market price in trading stock. While this has the effect of "leav[ing] individualized questions of reliance in the case," *post*, at 12, there is no reason to think that these questions will overwhelm common ones and render class certification inappropriate under *Rule 23(b)(3)*. That the defendant might attempt to pick off the occasional class member here or there through individualized rebuttal does not cause individual questions to predominate.

Finally, Halliburton and its *amici* contend that, by facilitating securities class actions, the *Basic* presumption produces a number of serious and harmful consequences. Such class actions, they say, allow plaintiffs to extort large settlements from defendants for meritless claims; punish innocent shareholders, who end up having to pay settlements and judgments; impose excessive costs on businesses; and consume a disproportionately large share of judicial resources. . . .

These concerns are more appropriately addressed to Congress, which has in fact responded, to some extent, to many of the issues raised by Halliburton and its *amici*. Congress has, for example, enacted the Private Securities Litigation Reform Act of 1995 (PSLRA), 109 Stat. 737, which sought to combat perceived abuses in securities litigation with heightened pleading requirements, limits on damages and attorney's fees, a "safe harbor" for certain kinds of statements, restrictions on the selection of lead plaintiffs in securities class actions, sanctions for frivolous litigation, and stays of discovery pending motions to dismiss. See *Amgen*, 568 U. S., at ___ (slip op., at 19-20). And to prevent plaintiffs from circumventing these restrictions by bringing securities class actions under state law in state court, Congress also enacted the Securities Litigation Uniform Standards Act of 1998, 112 Stat. 3227, which precludes many state law class actions alleging securities fraud. See *Amgen, supra*, at ___ (slip op., at 20). Such legislation demonstrates Congress's willingness to consider policy concerns of the sort that Halliburton says should lead us to overrule *Basic*.

III

Halliburton proposes two alternatives to overruling *Basic* that would alleviate what it regards as the decision's most serious flaws. The first alternative would require plaintiffs to prove that a defendant's misrepresentation actually affected the stock price—so-called "price impact" —in order to invoke the *Basic* presumption. It should not be enough, Halliburton contends, for plaintiffs to demonstrate the general efficiency of the market in which the stock traded. Halliburton's second proposed alternative would allow defendants to rebut the presumption of reliance with evidence of a *lack* of price impact, not only at the merits stage—which all agree defendants may already do—but also before class certification.

A

As noted, to invoke the *Basic* presumption, a plaintiff must prove that: (1) the alleged misrepresentations were publicly known, (2) they were material, (3) the stock traded in an efficient market, and (4) the plaintiff traded the stock between when the misrepresentations were made and when the truth was revealed. See *Basic, 485 U. S., at 248, n. 27; Amgen, supra,* at ___ (slip op., at 15). . . .

The first three prerequisites are directed at price impact—"whether the alleged misrepresentations affected the market price in the first place." *Halliburton I,* 563 U. S., at ___ (slip op., at 8). In the absence of price impact, *Basic*'s fraud-on-the-market theory and presumption of reliance collapse. The "fundamental premise" underlying the presumption is "that an investor presumptively relies on a misrepresentation so long as it was reflected in the market price at the time of his transaction." 563 U. S., at ___ (slip op., at 7). If it was not, then there is "no grounding for any contention that [the] investor[] indirectly relied on th[at] misrepresentation[] through [his] reliance on the integrity of the market price." *Amgen, supra,* at ___ (slip op., at 17).

Halliburton argues that since the *Basic* presumption hinges on price impact, plaintiffs should be required to prove it directly in order to invoke the presumption. Proving the presumption's prerequisites, which are at best an imperfect proxy for price impact, should not suffice.

Far from a modest refinement of the *Basic* presumption, this proposal would radically alter the required showing for the reliance element of the *Rule 10b-5* cause of action. What is called the *Basic* presumption actually incorporates two constituent presumptions: First, if a plaintiff shows that the defendant's misrepresentation was public and material and that the stock traded in a generally efficient market, he is entitled to a presumption that the misrepresentation affected the stock price. Second, if the plaintiff also shows that he purchased the stock at the market price during the relevant period, he is entitled to a further presumption that he purchased the stock in reliance on the defendant's misrepresentation.

By requiring plaintiffs to prove price impact directly, Halliburton's proposal would take away the first constituent presumption. Halliburton's argument for doing so is the same as its primary argument for overruling the *Basic* presumption altogether: Because market efficiency is not a yes-or-no proposition, a public, material misrepresentation might not affect a stock's price even in a generally efficient market. But as explained, *Basic* never suggested otherwise; that is why it affords defendants an opportunity to rebut the presumption by showing, among other things, that the particular misrepresentation at issue did not affect the stock's market price. For the same reasons we declined to completely jettison the *Basic* presumption, we decline to effectively jettison half of it by revising the prerequisites for invoking it.

B

Even if plaintiffs need not directly prove price impact to invoke the *Basic* presumption, Halliburton contends that defendants should at least be allowed to defeat the presumption at the class certification stage through evidence that the misrepresentation did not in fact affect the stock price. We agree.

1

There is no dispute that defendants may introduce such evidence at the merits stage to rebut the *Basic* presumption. *Basic* itself "made clear that the presumption was just that, and could be rebutted by appropriate evidence," including evidence that the asserted misrepresentation (or its correction) did not affect the market price of the defendant's stock. *Halliburton I, supra,* at ___ (slip op., at 5); see *Basic, supra, at 248.*

Nor is there any dispute that defendants may introduce price impact evidence at the class certification stage, so long as it is for the purpose of countering a plaintiff's showing of market efficiency, rather than directly rebutting the presumption. . . .

After all, plaintiffs themselves can and do introduce evidence of the *existence* of price impact in connection with "event studies" — regression analyses that seek to show that the market price of the defendant's stock tends to respond to pertinent publicly reported events. See Brief for Law Professors as *Amici Curiae* 25-28. In this case, for example, EPJ Fund submitted an event study of various episodes that might have been expected to affect the price of Halliburton's stock, in order to demonstrate that the market for that stock takes account of material, public information about the company. See App. 217-230 (describing the results of the study). The episodes examined by EPJ Fund's event study included one of the alleged misrepresentations that form the basis of the Fund's suit. . . .

Defendants—like plaintiffs—may accordingly submit price impact evidence prior to class certification. What defendants may not do, EPJ Fund insists and the Court of Appeals held, is rely on that same evidence prior to class certification for the particular purpose of rebutting the presumption altogether.

This restriction makes no sense, and can readily lead to bizarre results. Suppose a defendant at the certification stage submits an event study looking at the impact on the price of its stock from six discrete events, in an effort to refute the plaintiffs' claim of general market efficiency. All agree the defendant may do this. Suppose one of the six events is the specific misrepresentation asserted by the plaintiffs. All agree that this too is perfectly acceptable. Now suppose the district court determines that, despite the defendant's study, the plaintiff has carried its burden to prove market efficiency, but that the evidence shows no price impact with respect to the specific misrepresentation challenged in the suit. The evidence at the certification stage thus shows an efficient market, on which the alleged misrepresentation had no price impact. And yet under EPJ Fund's view, the plaintiffs' action should be certified and proceed as a class action (with all that entails), even though the fraud-on-the-market theory does not apply and common reliance thus cannot be presumed.

Such a result is inconsistent with *Basic*'s own logic. Under *Basic*'s fraud-on-the-market theory, market efficiency and the other prerequisites for invoking the presumption constitute an indirect way of showing price impact. As explained, it is appropriate to allow plaintiffs to rely on this indirect proxy for price impact, rather than requiring them to prove price impact directly, given *Basic*'s rationales for recognizing a presumption of reliance in the first place. . . .

But an indirect proxy should not preclude direct evidence when such evidence is available. As we explained in *Basic*, "[a]ny showing that severs the link between the alleged misrepresentation and . . . the price received (or paid) by the plaintiff . . . will be sufficient to rebut the presumption of reliance" because "the basis for finding that the fraud had been transmitted through market price would be gone." *485 U. S., at 248.* And without the presumption of reliance, a *Rule 10b-5* suit cannot proceed as a class action: Each plaintiff would have to prove reliance individually, so common issues would not "predominate" over individual ones, as required by *Rule 23(b)(3)*. *Id., at 242*. Price impact is thus an essential precondition for any *Rule 10b-5* class action. While *Basic* allows plaintiffs to establish that precondition indirectly, it does not require courts to ignore a defendant's direct, more salient evidence showing that the alleged misrepresentation did not actually affect the stock's market price and, consequently, that the *Basic* presumption does not apply.

2

The Court of Appeals relied on our decision in *Amgen* in holding that Halliburton could not introduce evidence of lack of price impact at the class certification stage. The question in *Amgen* was whether plaintiffs could be required to prove (or defendants be permitted to disprove) materiality before class certification. Even though materiality is a prerequisite for invoking the *Basic* presumption, we held that it should be left to the merits stage, because it does not bear on the predominance requirement of *Rule 23(b)(3)*. We reasoned that materiality is an objective issue susceptible to common, classwide proof. 568 U. S., at ___ (slip op., at 11). We also noted that a failure to prove materiality would necessarily defeat every plaintiff's claim on the merits; it would not simply preclude invocation of the presumption and thereby cause individual questions of reliance to predominate over common ones. *Ibid.* See also *id.,* at _____ (slip op., at 17-18). In this latter respect, we explained, materiality differs from the publicity and market efficiency prerequisites, neither of which is necessary to prove a *Rule 10b-5* claim on the merits. *Id.,* at ___, ___ (slip op., at 16-18).

EPJ Fund argues that much of the foregoing could be said of price impact as well. Fair enough. But price impact differs from materiality in a crucial respect. Given that the other *Basic* prerequisites must still be proved at the class certification stage, the common issue of materiality can be left to the merits stage without risking the certification of classes in which individual issues will end up overwhelming common ones. And because materiality is a discrete issue that can be resolved in isolation from the other prerequisites, it can be wholly confined to the merits stage.

Price impact is different. The fact that a misrepresentation "was reflected in the market price at the time of [the] transaction"—that it had price impact—is "*Basic*'s fundamental premise." *Halliburton I,* 563 U. S., at ___ (slip op., at 7). It thus has everything to do with the issue of predominance at the class certification stage. That is why, if reliance is to be shown through the *Basic* presumption, the publicity and market efficiency prerequisites must be proved before class certification. Without proof of those prerequisites, the fraud-on-the-market theory underlying the presumption completely collapses, rendering class certification inappropriate.

But as explained, publicity and market efficiency are nothing more than prerequisites for an indirect showing of price impact. There is no dispute that at least such indirect proof of price impact "is needed to ensure that the questions of law or fact common to the class will 'predominate.'"

. . . That is so even though such proof is also highly relevant at the merits stage.

Our choice in this case, then, is not between allowing price impact evidence at the class certification stage or relegating it to the merits. Evidence of price impact will be before the court at the certification stage in any event. The choice, rather, is between limiting the price impact inquiry before class certification to indirect evidence, or allowing consideration of direct evidence as well. As explained, we see no reason to artificially limit the inquiry at the certification stage to indirect evidence of price impact. Defendants may seek to defeat the *Basic* presumption at that stage through direct as well as indirect price impact evidence.

More than 25 years ago, we held that plaintiffs could satisfy the reliance element of the *Rule 10b-5* cause of action by invoking a presumption that a public, material misrepresentation will distort the price of stock traded in an efficient market, and that anyone who purchases the stock at the market price may be considered to have done so in reliance on the misrepresentation. We adhere to that decision and decline to modify the prerequisites for invoking the presumption of reliance. But to maintain the consistency of the presumption with the class certification requirements of *Federal Rule of Civil Procedure 23*, defendants must be afforded an opportunity before class certification to defeat the presumption through evidence that an alleged misrepresentation did not actually affect the market price of the stock.

Because the courts below denied Halliburton that opportunity, we vacate the judgment of the Court of Appeals for the Fifth Circuit and remand the case for further proceedings consistent with this opinion.

It is so ordered.

JUSTICE GINSBURG, with whom JUSTICE BREYER [*46] and JUSTICE SOTOMAYOR join, concurring.

Advancing price impact consideration from the merits stage to the certification stage may broaden the scope of discovery available at certification. . . . But the Court recognizes that it is incumbent upon the defendant to show the absence of price impact. . . . The Court's judgment, therefore, should impose no heavy toll on securities-fraud plaintiffs with tenable claims. On that understanding, I join the Court's opinion.

JUSTICE THOMAS, with whom JUSTICE SCALIA and JUSTICE ALITO join, concurring in the judgment.

. . .

Today we are asked to determine whether *Basic* was correctly decided. The Court suggests that it was, and that *stare decisis* demands that we preserve it. I disagree. Logic, economic realities, and our subsequent jurisprudence have undermined the foundations of the *Basic* presumption, and *stare decisis* cannot prop up the facade that remains. *Basic* should be overruled.

I

Understanding where *Basic* went wrong requires an explanation of the "reliance" requirement as traditionally understood.

. . .

The "traditional" reliance element requires a plaintiff to "sho[w] that he was aware of a company's statement and engaged in a relevant transaction . . . based on that specific misrepresentation." *Erica P. John Fund, supra,* at ___ (slip op., at 4). But investors who purchase stock from third parties on impersonal exchanges (*e.g.,* the New York Stock Exchange) often will not be aware of any particular statement made by the issuer of the security, and therefore cannot establish that they transacted based on a specific misrepresentation. Nor is the traditional reliance requirement amenable to class treatment; the inherently individualized nature of the reliance inquiry renders it impossible for a 10b-5 plaintiff to prove that common questions predominate over individual ones, making class certification improper. See *Basic, supra,* at 242; Fed. Rule Civ. Proc. 23(b)(3).

Citing these difficulties of proof and class certification, *485 U. S.,* at 242, 245, the *Basic* Court dispensed with the traditional reliance requirement in favor of a new one based on the fraud-on-the-market theory. . . .

II

Basic's reimagined reliance requirement was a mistake, and the passage of time has compounded its failings. First, the Court based both parts of the presumption of reliance on a questionable understanding of disputed economic theory and flawed intuitions about investor behavior. Second, *Basic*'s rebuttable presumption is at odds with our subsequent *Rule 23* cases, which require plaintiffs seeking class certification to " 'affirmatively demonstrate'" certification requirements like the predominance of common questions. *Comcast Corp.* v. *Behrend,* 569 U. S. ___, ___ (2013) (slip op., at 5) (quoting *Wal-Mart Stores, Inc.* v. *Dukes,* 564 U. S. ___, ___ (2011) (slip op., at 10)). Finally, *Basic*'s presumption that investors rely on the integrity of the market price is virtually irrebuttable in practice, which means that the "essential" reliance element effectively exists in name only.

A

Basic based the presumption of reliance on two factual assumptions. The first assumption was that, in a "well-developed market," public statements are generally "reflected" in the market price of securities. *485 U. S.,* at 247. The second was that investors in such markets transact "in reliance on the integrity of that price." *Ibid.* . . .

1

The Court's first assumption was that "most publicly available information" —including public misstatements—"is reflected in [the] market price" of a security. *Id., at 247.* The Court grounded that assumption in "empirical studies" testing a then-nascent economic theory known as the efficient capital markets hypothesis. *Id., at 246-247.* Specifically, the Court relied upon the "semi-strong" version of that theory, which posits that the average investor cannot earn above-market returns (*i.e.,* "beat the market") in an efficient market by trading on the basis of publicly available information. See, *e.g.,* Stout, The Mechanisms of Market Inefficiency: An Introduction to the New Finance, 28 J. Corp. L. 635, 640, and n. 24 (2003) (citing Fama, Efficient Capital Markets: A Review of Theory and Empirical Work, 25 J. Finance 383, 388 (1970)). The upshot of the hypothesis is that "the market price of shares traded on well-developed markets [will] reflec[t] all publicly available information, and, hence, any material misrepresentations." *Basic, supra, at 246.* At the time of *Basic,* this version of the efficient capital markets hypothesis was "widely accepted." See Dunbar & Heller 463-464.

This view of market efficiency has since lost its luster. See, *e.g.,* Langevoort, *Basic* at Twenty: Rethinking Fraud on the Market, *2009 Wis. L. Rev. 151, 175* ("Doubts about the strength and pervasiveness of market efficiency are much greater today than they were in the mid-1980s"). As it turns out, even "well-developed" markets (like the New York Stock Exchange) do not uniformly incorporate information into market prices with high speed. "[F]riction in accessing public information" and the presence of "processing costs" means that "not all public information will be impounded in a security's price with the same alacrity, or perhaps with any quickness at all." Cox, Understanding Causation in Private Securities Lawsuits: Building on *Amgen, 66 Vand. L. Rev. 1719, 1732 (2013)* (hereinafter Cox). For example, information that is easily digestible (merger announcements or stock splits) or especially prominent (Wall Street Journal articles) may be incorporated quickly, while information that is broadly applicable or technical (Securities and Exchange Commission filings) may be incorporated slowly or even ignored. See Stout, *supra,* at 653-656; see *e.g., In re Merck & Co. Securities Litigation, 432 F. 3d 261, 263-265 (CA3 2005)* (a Wall Street Journal article caused a steep decline in the company's stock price even though the same information was contained in an earlier SEC disclosure).

Further, and more importantly, "overwhelming empirical evidence" now suggests that even when markets do incorporate public information, they often fail to do so accurately. Lev and de Villiers, Stock Price Crashes and 10b-5 Damages: A Legal, Economic and Policy Analysis, *47 Stan. L. Rev. 7, 20-21 (1994)*; see also *id., at 21* ("That many share price movements seem unrelated to specific information strongly suggests that capital markets are not fundamentally efficient, and that wide deviations from fundamentals . . . can occur" (footnote omitted)). "Scores" of "efficiency-defying anomalies" —such as market swings in the absence of new information and prolonged deviations from underlying asset values—make market efficiency "more contestable than ever." Langevoort, Taming the Animal Spirits of the Stock Markets: A Behavioral Approach to Securities Regulation, *97 Nw. U. L. Rev. 135, 141 (2002)*; Dunbar & Heller 476-483. Such anomalies make it difficult to tell whether, at any given moment, a stock's price accurately reflects its value as indicated by all publicly available information. In sum, economists now understand that the price impact *Basic* assumed would happen reflexively is actually far from certain even in "well-developed" markets. Thus, *Basic*'s claim that "common sense and probability" support a presumption of reliance rests on shaky footing.

2

The *Basic* Court also grounded the presumption of reliance in a second assumption: that "[a]n investor who buys or sells stock at the price set by the market does so in reliance on the integrity of that price." *485 U. S., at 247.* In other words, the Court assumed that investors transact based on the belief that the market price accurately reflects the underlying " 'value' " of the security. See *id., at 244* (" '[P]urchasers generally rely on the price of the stock as a reflection of its value' "). . . .

It cannot be seriously disputed that a great many investors do *not* buy or sell stock based on a belief that the stock's price accurately reflects its value. Many investors in fact trade for the opposite reason—that is, because they think the market has under- or overvalued the stock, and they believe they can profit from that mispricing. *Id., at 256* (opinion of White, J.); see, *e.g.,* Macey, The Fraud on the Market Theory: Some Preliminary Issues, *74 Cornell L. Rev. 923, 925 (1989)* (The "opposite" of *Basic*'s assumption appears to be true; some investors "attempt to locate undervalued stocks in an effort to 'beat the market' . . . in essence betting that the market . . . is in fact inefficient"). Indeed, securities transactions often take place because the transacting parties disagree on the security's value. See, *e.g.,* Stout, Are Stock Markets Costly Casinos? Disagreement, Market Failure, and Securities Regulation, *81 Va. L. Rev. 611, 619 (1995)* ("[A]vailable evidence suggests that . . . investor disagreement inspires the lion's share of equities transactions").

Other investors trade for reasons entirely unrelated to price—for instance, to address changing liquidity needs, tax concerns, or portfolio balancing requirements. See *id., at 657-658*; see also Cox 1739 (investors may purchase "due to portfolio rebalancing arising from its obeisance to an indexing strategy"). These investment decisions—made with indifference to price and thus without regard for price "integrity" —are at odds with *Basic*'s understanding of what motivates investment decisions. In short, *Basic*'s assumption that all investors rely in common on "price integrity" is simply wrong.

The majority tries (but fails) to reconcile *Basic*'s assumption . . . on the more modest view that " '*most* investors' " rely on the integrity of a security's market price. . . . That gloss is difficult to square with *Basic*'s plain language: "An investor who buys or sells stock at the price set by the market does so in reliance on the integrity of that price." *Basic*, 458 U. S., at 247; see also *id., at 246-247* (" '[I]t is hard to imagine that there ever is a buyer or seller who does not rely on market integrity' "). . . .

The majority also suggests that "there is no reason to suppose" that investors who buy stock they believe to be undervalued are "indifferent to the integrity of market prices." . . . Such "value investor[s]," according to the majority, "implicitly rel[y] on the fact that a stock's market price will eventually reflect material information" and "presumably tr[y] to estimate *how* undervalued or overvalued a particular stock is" by reference to the market price. *Ibid.* Whether the majority's unsupported claims about the thought processes of hypothetical investors are accurate or not, they are surely beside the point. Whatever else an investor believes about the market, he simply does not "rely on the integrity of the market price" if he does not believe that the market price accurately reflects public information *at the time he transacts*. That is, an investor cannot claim that a public misstatement induced his transaction by distorting the market price if he did not buy at that price while believing that it accurately incorporated that public information. For that sort of investor, *Basic*'s critical fiction falls apart.

B

Basic's presumption of reliance also conflicts with our more recent cases clarifying *Rule 23*'s class-certification requirements. Those cases instruct that "a party seeking to maintain a class action 'must affirmatively demonstrate his compliance' with *Rule 23*." *Comcast*, 569 U. S., at ___ (slip op., at 5) (quoting *Wal-Mart*, 564 U. S., at ___ (slip op., at 10). To prevail on a motion for class certification, a party must demonstrate through "evidentiary proof" that " 'questions of law or fact common to class members predominate over any questions affecting only individual members.' " 569 U. S., at ___ (slip op., at 5-6). . . .

Basic thus exempts *Rule 10b-5* plaintiffs from *Rule 23*'s proof requirement. Plaintiffs who invoke the presumption of reliance are deemed to have shown predominance as a matter of law, even though the resulting rebuttable presumption leaves individualized questions of reliance in the case and predominance still unproved. Needless to say, that exemption was beyond the *Basic* Court's power to grant.

C

It would be bad enough if *Basic* merely provided an end-run around *Rule 23*. But in practice, the so-called "rebuttable presumption" is largely irrebuttable.

The *Basic* Court ostensibly afforded defendants an opportunity to rebut the presumption by providing evidence that either aspect of a plaintiff's fraud-on-the-market reliance—price impact, or reliance on the integrity of the market price—is missing. *485 U. S., at 248-249.* As it turns out, however, the realities of class-action procedure make rebuttal based on an individual plaintiff's lack of reliance virtually impossible. At the class-certification stage, rebuttal is only directed at the class representatives, which means that counsel only needs to find one class member who can withstand the challenge. See Grundfest, Damages and Reliance Under *Section 10(b)* of the Exchange Act, *69 Bus. Lawyer 307, 362 (2014).* After class certification, courts have refused to allow defendants to challenge any plaintiff's reliance on the integrity of the market price prior to a determination on classwide liability. See Brief for Chamber of Commerce of the United States of America et al. as *Amici Curiae* 13-14 (collecting cases rejecting post-certification attempts to rebut individual class members' reliance on price integrity as not pertinent to classwide liability). One search for rebuttals on individual-reliance grounds turned up only six cases out of the thousands of *Rule 10b-5* actions brought since *Basic.* Grundfest, *supra,* at 360.

. . . Because the presumption is conclusive in practice with respect to investors' reliance on price integrity, even *Basic*'s watered-down reliance requirement has been effectively eliminated. . . .

For these reasons, *Basic* should be overruled in favor of the straightforward rule that "[r]eliance by the plaintiff upon the defendant's deceptive acts "—actual reliance, not the fictional "fraud-on-the-market" version—"is an essential element of the *§10(b)* private cause of action." *Stoneridge, 552 U. S., at 159.*

. . .

NOTE

While *Halliburton* is most notable for sustaining the fraud-on-the-market theory, its conclusion that defendants may seek to rebut plaintiffs' claim that the fraud distorted the market price as part of class certification (i.e., at the outset of the litigation, rather than waiting for trial). In many cases, plaintiffs argue that but for the fraud, the stock price would have dropped, but because of it, the price was "maintained" at an artificially high level. If so, there would be no obvious evidence of distortion. Courts are only now coming to address what should happen in the face of maintenance claims. In *IBEW Local 98 v. Best Buy Inc.*, 2016 WL 1425807 (8th Cir. 2016), the Eighth Circuit accepted defendant's no impact argument based on the lack of price movement because *plaintiffs* had not introduced affirmative proof of maintenance. The dissenting judge said that this misreads *Halliburton*, and puts plaintiffs to an impossible task. The factual posture of the case was somewhat unusual because, according to the trial judge, Best Buy's initial misstatement in a press release *did* cause a noticeable stock price drop but was protected from liability by the PSLRA's safe harbor for forward looking information. Thus plaintiffs were left to argue maintenance based on management's unprotected reiteration of the same guidance in a conference call later the same day.

‖14‖

The Enforcement
of the Securities Laws

**A. More on the Private Enforcement of the
     Securities Laws**

**3. Closing the Bypass: The Securities Litigation Uniform
     Standards Act**

**Page 794.   Add the following case at the end of the carryover
               paragraph at the top of the page:**

‖ **Chadbourne & Parke LLP v. Troice**
‖ **134 S. Ct. 1058 (2014)**

JUSTICE BREYER delivered the opinion of the Court. . . .

B

1

The plaintiffs in these actions (respondents here) say that Allen
Stanford and several of his companies ran a multibillion dollar Ponzi
scheme. Essentially, Stanford and his companies sold the plaintiffs certificates of deposit in Stanford International Bank. Those certificates "were
debt assets that promised a fixed rate of return." *Roland* v. *Green*, 675 F. 3d

503, 522 (CA5 2012). The plaintiffs expected that Stanford International Bank would use the money it received to buy highly lucrative assets. But instead, Stanford and his associates used the money provided by new investors to repay old investors, to finance an elaborate lifestyle, and to finance speculative real estate ventures.

The Department of Justice brought related criminal charges against Allen Stanford. A jury convicted Stanford of mail fraud, wire fraud, conspiracy to commit money laundering, and obstruction of a Securities and Exchange Commission investigation. Stanford was sentenced to prison and required to forfeit $6 billion. The SEC, noting that the Bank certificates of deposit fell within the 1934 Securities Exchange Act's broad definition of "security," filed a §10(b) civil case against Allen Stanford, the Stanford International Bank, and related Stanford companies and associates. The SEC won the civil action, and the court imposed a civil penalty of $6 billion.

2

The plaintiffs in each of the four civil class actions are private investors who bought the Bank's certificates of deposit. . . .

The defendants in each of the cases moved to dismiss the complaints. . . . The court recognized that the certificates of deposit themselves were not "covered securities" under the Litigation Act, for they were not " 'traded nationally [or] listed on a regulated national exchange.' " App. to Pet. for Cert. in No. 12-86, p. 62. But each complaint in one way or another alleged that the fraud included misrepresentations that the Bank maintained significant holdings in " 'highly marketable securities issued by stable governments [and] strong multinational companies,' " and that the Bank's ownership of these "covered" securities made investments in the uncovered certificates more secure. *Id.*, at 66. The court concluded that this circumstance provided the requisite statutory "connection" between (1) the plaintiffs' state-law fraud claims, and (2) "transactions in covered securities." *Id.*, at 64, 66-67. Hence, the court dismissed the class actions under the Litigation Act. . . .

The Fifth Circuit reversed. . . . The court held that the falsehoods about the Bank's holdings in covered securities were too " 'tangentially related' " to the "crux" of the fraud to trigger the Litigation Act. . . . We granted their petitions.

II

The question before us concerns the scope of the Litigation Act's phrase "misrepresentation or omission of a material fact in connection with the purchase or sale of a covered security." §78bb(f)(1)(A). How broad is that scope? Does it extend further than misrepresentations that are material to the purchase or sale of a covered security?

In our view, the scope of this language does not extend further. To put the matter more specifically: A fraudulent misrepresentation or omission is not made "in connection with" such a "purchase or sale of a covered security" unless it is material to a decision by one or more individuals (other than the fraudster) to buy or to sell a "covered security." . . .

A

We reach this interpretation of the Litigation Act for several reasons. First, the Act focuses upon transactions in covered securities, not upon transactions in uncovered securities. An interpretation that insists upon a material connection with a transaction in a covered security is consistent with the Act's basic focus.

Second, a natural reading of the Act's language supports our interpretation. The language requires the dismissal of a state-law-based class action where a private party alleges a "misrepresentation or omission of a material fact" (or engages in other forms of deception, not relevant here) "in connection with the purchase or sale of a covered security." §78bb(f)(1). The phrase "material fact in connection with the purchase or sale" suggests a connection that matters. And for present purposes, a connection matters where the misrepresentation makes a significant difference to someone's decision to purchase or to sell a covered security, not to purchase or to sell an uncovered security, something about which the Act expresses no concern. . . . Further, the "someone" making that decision to purchase or sell must be a party other than the fraudster. If the only party who decides to buy or sell a covered security as a result of a lie is the liar, that is not a "connection" that matters.

Third, prior case law supports our interpretation. As far as we are aware, every securities case in which this Court has found a fraud to be "in connection with" a purchase or sale of a security has involved victims who took, who tried to take, who divested themselves of, who tried to divest themselves of, or who maintained *an ownership interest* in financial instruments that fall within the relevant statutory definition. See, *e.g., Dabit, supra,* at 77, 126 S. Ct. 1503, 164 L. Ed. 2d 179 (Litigation Act: victims were "holders" of covered securities that the defendant's fraud caused to become overvalued); *SEC* v. *Zandford,* 535 U. S. 813, 822, 122 S. Ct. 1899, 153 L. Ed. 2d 1 (2002) §10(b): victims were "duped into believing" that the defendant would " 'invest' their assets in the stock market"); *Wharf (Holdings) Ltd.* v. *United Int'l Holdings, Inc.,* 532 U. S. 588, 592, 121 S. Ct. 1776, 149 L. Ed. 2d 845 (2001) (§10(b): victim purchased an oral option to buy 10% of a company's stock); *O'Hagan, supra,* at 655-656, 117 S. Ct. 2199, 138 L. Ed.

2d 724 (§10(b): victims were "members of the investing public" harmed by the defendant's "gain[ing of an] advantageous market position" through insider trading); *Superintendent of Ins. of N. Y. v. Bankers Life & Casualty Co.*, 404 U. S. 6, 10, 92 S. Ct. 165, 30 L. Ed. 2d 128 (1971) (§10(b): victim was "injured as an investor" when the fraud deprived it of "compensation for the sale of its valuable block of securities"). We have found no Court case involving a fraud "in connection with" the purchase or sale of a statutorily defined security in which the victims did not fit one of these descriptions. And the dissent apparently has not either.

. . .

Fourth, we read the Litigation Act in light of and consistent with the underlying regulatory statutes, the Securities Exchange Act of 1934 and the Securities Act of 1933. The regulatory statutes refer to persons engaged in securities transactions that lead to the taking or dissolving of ownership positions. And they make it illegal to deceive a person when he or she is doing so. Section 5 of the 1933 Act, for example, makes it unlawful to "offer to sell or offer to buy . . . any security, unless a registration statement has been filed as to such security." 15 U. S. C. §77e(c). Section 17 of the 1933 Act makes it unlawful "in the offer or sale of any securities . . . to employ any device, scheme, or artifice to defraud, or to obtain money or property by means of any untrue statement of a material fact." §§77q(a)(1)-(2). And §10(b) of the 1934 Act makes it unlawful to "use or employ, in connection with the purchase or sale of any security . . . any manipulative or deceptive device or contrivance." §78j(b).

Not only language but also purpose suggests a statutory focus upon transactions involving the statutorily relevant securities. . . . Nothing in the regulatory statutes suggests their object is to protect persons whose connection with the statutorily defined securities is more remote than words such as "buy," "sell," and the like, indicate. Nor does anything in the Litigation Act provide us with reasons for interpreting its similar language more broadly.

. . .

Fifth, to interpret the necessary statutory "connection" more broadly than we do here would interfere with state efforts to provide remedies for victims of ordinary state-law frauds. A broader interpretation would allow the Litigation Act to cover, and thereby to prohibit, a lawsuit brought by creditors of a small business that falsely represented it was creditworthy, in part because it owns or intends to own exchange-traded stock. It could prohibit a lawsuit brought by homeowners against a mortgage broker for lying about the interest rates on their mortgages – if, say, the broker (not the homeowners) later sold the mortgages to a bank which then securitized them in a pool and sold off pieces as "covered securities." Brief for Sixteen Law Professors as *Amici Curiae* 24. . . .

B

. . . [T]he Government points out that §10(b) of the Securities Exchange Act also uses the phrase "in connection with the purchase or sale of any security." 15 U. S. C. §78j(b). And the Government warns that a narrow interpretation of "in connection with" here threatens a similarly narrow interpretation there, which could limit the SEC's enforcement capabilities. See Brief for United States as *Amicus Curiae* 28.

We do not understand, however, how our interpretation could significantly curtail the SEC's enforcement powers. As far as the Government has explained the matter, our interpretation seems perfectly consistent with past SEC practice. For one thing, we have cast no doubt on the SEC's ability to bring enforcement actions against Stanford and Stanford International Bank. The SEC has already done so successfully. As we have repeatedly pointed out, the term "security" under §10(b) covers a wide range of financial products beyond those traded on national exchanges, apparently including the Bank's certificates of deposit at issue in these cases. No one here denies that, for §10(b) purposes, the "material" misrepresentations by Stanford and his associates were made "in connection with" the "purchases" of those certificates.

We find it surprising that the dissent worries that our decision will "narro[w] and constric[t] essential protection for our national securities market," *post*, at 3, and put "frauds like the one here . . . not within the reach of federal regulation," . . . That would be news to Allen Stanford, who was sentenced to 110 years in federal prison after a successful federal prosecution, and to Stanford International Bank, which was ordered to pay billions in federal fines, after the same. Frauds like the one here – including *this fraud itself*– will continue to be within the reach of federal regulation because the authority of the SEC and Department of Justice extends to all "securities," not just to those traded on national exchanges. 15 U. S. C. §78c(a)(10); accord, §77b(a)(1), §80a-2(a)(36), §80b-2(a)(18). When the fraudster peddles an uncovered security like the CDs here, the Federal Government will have the full scope of its usual powers to act. The only difference between our approach and that of the dissent, is that we *also* preserve the ability for investors to obtain relief under state laws when the fraud bears so remote a connection to the national securities market that no person actually believed he was taking an ownership position in that market.

Thus, despite the Government's and the dissent's hand wringing, neither has been able to point to an example of any prior SEC enforcement action brought during the past 80 years that our holding today would have prevented the SEC from bringing. . . .

For these reasons the Court of Appeals' judgment is affirmed.

It is so ordered.

JUSTICE THOMAS, concurring.

We have said that the statutory phrase "in connection with" warrants a "broad interpretation," *Merrill Lynch, Pierce, Fenner & Smith Inc.* v. *Dabit*, 547 U. S. 71, 85, 126 S. Ct. 1503, 164 L. Ed. 2d 179 (2006), though not so broad as to reach any "common-law . . . fraud that happens to involve securities," see *SEC* v. *Zandford*, 535 U. S. 813, 820, 122 S. Ct. 1899, 153 L. Ed. 2d 1 (2002. . . . As I understand it, the opinion of the Court resolves this case by applying a limiting principle to the phrase "in connection with" that is "consistent with the statutory framework and design" of the Securities Litigation Uniform Standards Act of 1998 . . . and also consistent with our precedents.

JUSTICE KENNEDY, with whom JUSTICE ALITO joins, dissenting.

. . .

This litigation is very similar to *Zandford* and satisfies the coincides test it sets forth, and for similar reasons. In *Zandford*, the SEC brought a civil action against a broker, who, over a period of time, gained control of an investment account, sold its securities, and then pocketed the proceeds. 535 U. S., at 815-816, 122 S. Ct. 1899, 153 L. Ed. 2d 1. The broker argued that "the sales themselves were perfectly lawful and that the subsequent misappropriation of the proceeds, though fraud-lent, is not properly viewed as having the requisite connection with the sales." *Id.*, at 820, 122 S. Ct. 1899, 153 L. Ed. 2d 1. The Court rejected that argument. Although the transactions were lawful and separate from the misappropriations, the two were "not independent events." *Ibid.* Rather, the fraud "coincided with the sales," in part because the sales "further[ed]" the fraud. *Ibid.*

The Court likened the broker's fraud to that in *Superintendent of Ins. of N. Y.* v. *Bankers Life & Casualty Co.*, 404 U. S. 6, 10, 92 S. Ct. 165, 30 L. Ed. 2d 128 (1971), where the fraud victims were misled to believe that they "would receive the proceeds of the sale" of securities. *Zandford*, 535 U. S., at 821, 122 S. Ct. 1899, 153 L. Ed. 2d 1. Like the victims in *Bankers Life*, the victims in *Zandford* "were injured as investors through [the broker]'s deceptions" because "[t]hey were duped into believing that [the broker] would 'conservatively invest' their assets in the stock market and that any transactions made on their behalf would be for their benefit." *Id.*, at 822, 122 S. Ct. 1899, 153 L. Ed. 2d 1. Both suffered losses because they were victims of dishonest intermediaries or fiduciaries. See also *In re Richard J. Line*, 62 S.E.C. Docket 2879, 1996 SEC LEXIS 2746 (1996) (broker who induced parents to transfer funds to him to invest in securities so as to temporarily hide them during the college financial aid application process, but then failed to return the money, violated Rule 10b-5).

Here, just as in *Zandford*, the victims parted with their money based on a fraudster's promise to invest it on their behalf by purchases and sales in the securities markets. The investors had – or were led to believe they could have – the advantages of Stanford's and SIB's expertise in investments in the national market. So here, as in *Zandford*, the success of the fraud turned on the promise to trade in regulated securities. According to the complaints, SIB represented that it would " 'reinves[t]' " the plaintiffs' money on their behalf in "a well-diversified portfolio of highly marketable securities issued by stable national governments, strong multinational companies, and major international banks" to ensure a "safe, liquid," and above-market return. . . . The misrepresentation was about nationally traded securities and lent credence to SIB's promise that the CDs were a liquid investment that "could be redeemed with just a few days' notice." . . . The CDs, SIB explained, would be backed by nationally traded securities. As a result, according to the complaints, the misrepresentation was "material." . . . The fraud could not have succeeded without the misrepresentation: The investors gave SIB money because they expected it to be invested in the national securities markets. The connection between the promised purchases and the misrepresentation is more direct than in *Zandford*, because the misrepresentation was essential to the fraud.

Here, and again just as in *Zandford*, the fraud was not complete until the representation about securities transactions became untrue, just as Stanford intended all along. Instead of purchasing covered securities, SIB purchased some but fewer covered securities than it promised – only 10% of its portfolio, according to an affidavit attached to a complaint – and primarily speculated in Caribbean real estate. . . . It was not until SIB rendered the CDs illiquid by failing to make substantial investments in the nationally traded securities it promised that the fraud was consummated. At that point, SIB blocked the plaintiffs' access to the market. The fraud and SIB's failure to purchase all that it promised were not independent events. Rather, the false promises to invest in covered securities enabled and furthered the CD fraud. Without the false promise, there would have been no money to purchase the covered securities. On these facts, this Court's controlling precedents instruct that these misrepresentations were made "in connection with the purchase or sale" of regulated securities; and, as a result, state-law claims concerning them should be precluded. . . .

G.   *Enforcement Actions by the SEC*

1.   Investigations

b.   *Recommendations to the Commission*

Page 838.   Add the following to Note 2:

Professor Amanda Rose has reasoned that a potential consequence of the whistleblower program's bounty to insiders and others who report wrong-doing to the SEC is to remove this source of information from class action lawyers with the consequential effect that we might see not only a rise in SEC enforcement suits and a concomitant decline in private securities class actions. *See* Rose, Better Bounty Hunting: How the SEC's New Whistleblower Program Changes the Securities Fraud Class Action Debate, 108 Nw. U. L. Rev. 1235 (2014).

2.   Sanctioning in SEC Enforcement Proceedings

a.   *The Administrative Enforcement Proceeding*

Page 842. Insert the following at the end of the subsection:

In recent years, an increasing percentage of SEC enforcement actions have been before administrative law judges and not in the federal courts. This has prompted numerous constitutional due process challenges to SEC procedures (there being possible internal bias on the part of presiding administrative law judges) as well as whether respondents have a constitu-tional right to defend their conduct before a federal court. Such challenges have with some consistency been unsuccessful. The more formidable chal-lenge, however, is whether the SEC's procedures for appointing its admin-istrative law judges violate the Appointments Clause of Article II of the Constitution. SEC administrative law judges are appointed by the Office of Personnel Management, not by the commissioners or by the Chairman of the SEC. The constitutional issue is whether SEC administrative law judges wield such power that they are "inferior officers" so that their appointment per the Constitution must be by the President, the Congress, or the head of a department. An important early decision, *Hill v. Securities and Exchange Commission,* 114 F. Supp. 3d 1297 (N.D. Ga. 2015), held the process for appointing SEC administrative law violated the Constitution. *Hill* reached its conclusion by applying the Supreme Court's holding in *Freytag v. Comm'r Internal Revenue Service,* 501 U.S. 868 (1991) that a special trial judge in a

Tax Court was an inferior officer because he exercised "significant author-ity." Finding that the SEC's ALJs similarly wielded "significant authority," the *Hill* court concluded that the SEC's ALJs are inferior officers under Article II of the Constitution. Subsequent district court, and the few circuit court, decisions have neither accepted nor rejected *Hill*; instead the courts have dismissed direct challenges to the SEC's procedures, such as that made in *Hill*, holding instead that a respondent to an SEC administrative enforcement action must first raise any constitutional challenges before the administrative law judge.

b.   *The Panoply of SEC Enforcement Sanctions*

Page 849.   Add the following to the end of the first paragraph of Note 2:

A detailed analysis of 243 fair funds created between 2002 and 2013 that aggregated $14.46 billion found that in more than half the cases inves-tors "did not receive compensation in parallel securities litigation, either because no private action was filed or because the litigation became victim to one of the PSLRA screens. As a result, in a majority of fair fund cases, the fair fund is the only source of investor compensation." Velinkonja, Public Compensation for Private Harm: Evidence from the SEC's Fair Fund Distributions, 67 Stan. L. Rev. 331, 371 (2015).

3.   Injunctions

Page 861.   Add the following to the end of Note 9:

In *SEC v. Citigroup Global Markets, Inc.*, 752 F.3d 285, 294 (2nd Cir. 2014), the Second Circuit reversed Judge Rakoff, reasoning that, absent substan-tial basis in the record for concluding that the proposed settlement was not fair, was unreasonable or would disserve the public interest, the district court is required to enter an order consistent with the settlement's terms (while recognizing that in *private* settlement the court is to consider the additional factor of the settlement's adequacy). In the course of overruling Judge Rakoff the Second Circuit observed, perhaps cynically, "Trials are primarily about truth. Consent decrees are primarily about pragmatism."

10. Bad Actor and Ineligible Issuer Waivers.   Multiple regulatory dispensa-tions under the securities laws, such as the Rule 506 safe harbor for non-public offerings or those associated with being a well-known seasoned issuer, are not available to those who are the subject of an SEC or court order or criminal conviction arising from a securities enforcement action. Because bad actor and ineligible issuer provisions can add immensely to the consequences of an individual or firm violating the securities laws, respondents frequently request the SEC to exercise its authority to grant a waiver of such disqualification by showing good cause. In considering whether good cause exists for a waiver the Division of Corporate Finance considers the following: the nature of the violation, who was responsible for the misconduct, duration of the misconduct, remedial action taken by the party, and likely impact if a waiver request is denied. *See e.g.,* Credit Suisse AG, SEC No Action Letter [2014 Transfer Binder] Fed. Sec. L. Rep. (CCH) ¶ 77,704 (May 19, 2014) (having settled charges that it facilitated tax fraud that thereby triggered various bad actor disqualifiers, SEC granted waiver with respect to about 40 entities controlled by Credit Suisse on the justification the entities had not themselves engaged in the unlawful practice).

Professor Urska Velikonja reports that of the 201 waivers that were granted from July 2003 through 2014, 82 percent were to large financial firms (92 percent if we add large non-financial firms) and two-thirds of the waiver grants were in connection with violations involving multiple enforcement actions; waivers rarely occur in matters involving accounting fraud. Velikonja, Waiving Disqualification: When Do Securities Violators Receive a Reprieve? 103 Cal. L. Rev. 1081 (2015). Because there is no data gathered by the SEC regarding waiver requests, it is difficult to discern clearer patterns with respect to likely SEC heuristics in granting waivers. With a now growing awareness of waivers, and an ensuing debate of the practice, Professor Velikonja's data reflects that the frequency of waiver grants is trending downward.

||15||

The Regulation
of Insider Trading

E. Tippers and Tippees

1. Tipper/Tippee Liability Defined

Page 932.   Add the following after note 4:

5. Retrenchment?   In the context of a criminal prosecution of a third and a fourth level remote tippee (both portfolio managers at hedge funds), the Second Circuit arguably heightened the standard for liability under *Dirks*. United States v. Newman, 773 F.3d 438 (2d Cir. 2014). It held that when tippers are alleged to make a "gift" of the information, there must be "a meaningfully close personal relationship that generates an exchange that is objective, consequential, and represents at least a potential gain of a pecuniary or similarly valuable nature." Id. at 452. It also held that the tippee must *know* of that personal benefit. Finding evidence of both of these lacking because the two mid-level corporate insider/tippers had little to gain from passing on the confidential earnings information, the court overturned the convictions. Is the court's approach a fair reading of *Dirks*? In contrast, the Ninth Circuit rejected *Newman's* definition of a gift-based tip in a case where a young Citibank banker gave valuable secrets to his older brother, who in turn gave them to a friend (and soon, in-law), Salman. United States v. Salman, 792 F.3d 1087 (9th Cir. 2015). The analyst, who had pled guilty to the tipping, testified at trial that he did so out of love and affection for his brother. There was also evidence that Salman knew how the information had come to him. The court refused to read *Dirks* to require any pecuniary motivation with respects to gifts of information, and was troubled by the loophole that would be created were tips lawful simply because the tipper "asked for no tangible compensation in return." Id. at 1094. In early 2016, the Supreme Court granted certiorari in the *Salman* case to deal with the conflict between the circuits.

‖16‖

Shareholder Voting and Going-Private Transactions

A. The Election of Directors and Other Routine Matters

2. Proposals, Recommendations and Elections

Page 959.   After the second paragraph, insert the following:

In *Trinity Church Wall Street v. Wal-Mart Stores, Inc.*, 792 F.3d 323 (3d Cir. 2015), the court ruled that Wal-Mart could exclude a shareholder proposal asking the board of directors to amend the Governance Committee charter to provide for oversight and reporting of policies and standards for determining whether Wal-Mart should sell dangerous or offensive products. Though not singled out in the proposal, the shareholders' immediate concern was with Wal-Mart's sale of high capacity firearms like the Bushmaster AR-15. The proponents believed this raised an issue of social, moral and political importance, and so was not excludable under the "ordinary business" exemption. The court disagreed, holding that although such significance might take the proposal out of ordinary business if it is sufficiently "transcendent," the company can exclude by demonstrating that the issue is nonetheless so deeply enmeshed in basic business decision-making that it improperly treads on a core management responsibility, like creating an optimal product mix in the face of shifting consumer demand. Query: Would the proponents have been better off limiting their proposal to high-powered weapons?

C.   "Solicitations"

Page 971.   In place of Problem 16-2 insert:

The former CEO of a company wrote the following letter to company shareholders:

Dear Shareholder,

My name is Richard M. Osborne, former Chairman and CEO of Gas Natural Inc. After saving the company from near bankruptcy, I was tossed out because the attorney of our Derivative Lawsuit told our board members it would be the easiest way to settle. Mark Kratz, Gas Natural's current Securities Attorney who represented me personally for 35 years and Mike Victor, Chairman of the Compensation Committee, promised me three years severance for wrongful discharge. They later reneged on this promise. Lawsuits are in process for the $750,000 owed to me in earn-outs. I am also owed a minimum of $5,250,000 for pipelines they have been using illegally.

The company is now being run by accountants. It is a disaster and employee morale is at an all time low. Those in charge believe they can make a difference by pushing buttons. At the June 25th board meeting, cash flow was a cause for concern. I suggested we take the Directors Fees from $5,000 to $2,000 to help in this matter. The directors instead chose to milk the company and instead of giving the money to the share holders [sic] by granting themselves each 4,000 shares, the equivalent of $44,000 per director. Another example of their antics, during the only meeting I ever missed due to a surgery in 2013, the remaining board members raised the Directors Fees from $2,000 to $4,000.

I am asking for your help in running these greedy individuals out of our company. You will receive additional letters from me in the future. If you have your own concerns or complaints, please address them to me in writing to my office or directly . . . .

Would this be a proxy solicitation? Exempt? Protected by the First Amendment? See Gas Natural Inc. v. Osborne, 624 Fed. Appx. 944 (6th Cir. 2015).

||18||
Regulation of Broker-Dealers

B. The Responsibilities of Brokers to their Customers

1. The Broker as Agent: Fiduciary Obligations and the Shingle Theory

b. Advice and Recommendations

Page 1033. At the end of the first full paragraph, add:

As of early 2016, the SEC had not yet acted on the Dodd-Frank mandate. The Department of Labor did, however, move into that space in an effort to bring greater fiduciary responsibility to the brokerage and advisory industries. For some time, the Employee Retirement Income Security Act (ERISA) has imposed fiduciary responsibilities on those who give investment advice with respect to retirement accounts. But the existing definition of an advisory relationship was narrow. The DOL came to believe that many investors were being abused by being steered into high cost investments in their Individual Retirement Accounts and similar tax-deferred arrangements that benefitted the adviser more than the client. So, in the spring of 2016 the DOL dramatically expanded the definition of advisory relationships and recommendations so as to encompass under ERISA a far larger range of accounts that had theretofore only been subject to securities regulation. Because of the strict conflict of interest prohibitions of ERISA, brokers will have to change their practices considerably in order to fit into a new "Best Interest Contract" exemption regime that is a broad mix of principles-based duties and highly specific obligations. Of particular interest is the DOL's determination that private litigation should be a (if not the) primary enforcement mechanism for the fiduciary principles embedded in the new regime. ERISA creates powerful private rights of action, and the new DOL rules ban any exculpatory language in covered contracts, any requirement of remote arbitration venues, and any class action waivers in arbitration agreements. All of this is immensely controversial, with the industry threatening litigation to strike down the new rules and saying that they will have to drop smaller accounts where the fees are not sizable enough to justify the increased regulatory burdens and litigation risk. The SEC, in turn, has been criticized for not taking on the Dodd-Frank project in a way that might have caused the DOL to defer or at least coordinate with the SEC in a generalized approach to the obligations of broker-dealers and investment advisers in all investment settings.

|20|

Transnational Securities Fraud and the Reach of U.S. Securities Laws

A. The Extraterritorial Application of U.S. Securities Laws

3. Morrison Applied

NOTES AND QUESTIONS

Page 1136. Add the following new notes:

5. Morrison and Criminal Liability under Section 10(b). *Morrison* left open the question of whether limits on extraterritorial application of Section 10(b) apply in prosecutions seeking to establish criminal rather than civil liability under the section. In United States v. Vilar, 729 F.3d 62, 72 (2nd Cir. 2013), the Second Circuit stated "we have no problem concluding that *Morrison's* holding applies equally to criminal actions." In so ruling, the court pointed to the general presumption that criminal statutes are not applied extraterritorially, adding that Section 10(b) is no exception.

6. And What of Section 17(a)? Recall that Section 17(a) of the '33 Act is broader than Section 10(b) in that it reaches not just a sale but also an offer of securities. How, then, is *Morrison* to be applied when the alleged fraud is in the offer rather than the sale? The issue was addressed in *SEC v. Tourre*, 2013 U.S. Dist. LEXIS 78297 (S.D.N.Y. 2013), where the question for summary judgment purposes was whether certain marketing activities that took place in the United States are sufficient to render the fraud actionable under Section 17(a). In concluding *Morrison* does not bar the SEC's Section 17(a) claims, the court emphasized the important distinction

between Section 10(b)'s prohibition of fraud "in connection with the purchase or sale of any security" and Section 17(a)'s prohibition of fraud "in
the offer or sale" of any securities.

> That distinction is key. Section 17(a)'s proscription extends beyond
> consummated transactions. . . . Because Section 17(a) is not exclusively con-
> cerned with fraudulent conduct in connection with a transaction in securi-
> ties, but rather is concerned with such conduct in either the offer or the sale
> of securities, the requirement of domestic conduct under Section 17(a) must
> be extended accordingly. This means that a domestic offer may be actionable
> regardless of whether it results in a sale. *Morrison's* requirement of domestic
> conduct is necessarily applied individually and independently to each type of
> potential violation of Section 17(a).